THE FAMILY PRAYER BOOK

THE FAMILY PRAYER BOOK

COUNCIL FOR
MARRIAGE AND THE FAMILY
OF THE IRISH EPISCOPAL CONFERENCE

VERITAS

First published 2013 by
Veritas Publications
7–8 Lower Abbey Street
Dublin 1
publications@veritas.ie
www.veritas.ie

ISBN 978 1 84730 521 3

10 9 8 7 6 5 4 3 2

A catalogue record for this book is available from the British Library.

Every effort has been made to trace copyright holders and to obtain their
permission for the use of copyright material. Should any errors or
omissions occur, please notify the publisher and corrections will be
incorporated in any future reprints or editions of this book.

Imprimatur: ✠ Most Rev Diarmuid Martin,
Archbishop of Dublin
Given at Dublin this 6th day of August 2013

Designed by Colette Dower, Veritas Publications
Printed in the Republic of Ireland by Anglo Printers Ltd,
Drogheda

*Veritas books are printed on paper made from the wood pulp of managed
forests. For every tree felled, at least one tree is planted, thereby renewing
natural resources.*

THIS BOOK IS PRESENTED

TO _____

FROM _____

DATE _____

'Glory be to the Father, and to the Son,
and to the Holy Spirit.
As it was in the beginning, is now, and ever shall be,
world without end. Amen.'

Prayer for the Act of Consecration of Ireland to the Immaculate Heart of Mary

Most Blessed Virgin Mary, Mother of God and Refuge of Sinners, we entrust and consecrate ourselves, our family, our home, our dioceses and Ireland our country to Jesus through your Immaculate Heart. As your children, we promise to follow your example in our lives by doing at all times the will of God.

O Mary, Spouse of the Holy Spirit, we renew today the promises of our Baptism and Confirmation. Intercede for us with the Holy Spirit that we may be always faithful to your Divine Son, to his Mystical Body, the Catholic Church, and to the teachings of his Vicar on earth, our Holy Father the Pope.

Immaculate Heart of Mary, our Queen and our Mother, we promise to uphold the sanctity of marriage and the welfare of the family. Watch over our minds and hearts and preserve our young people from dangers to their faith and the many temptations that threaten them in the world today.

We ask you, Mary our Advocate, to intercede with your divine Son. Obtain for our country the grace to uphold the uniqueness of every human life, from the first moment of conception to natural death.

O Blessed Mother, Our Life, Our Sweetness and Our Hope, we wish that this Consecration be for the greater glory of God and that it lead us safely to Jesus your Son.

A Naomh-Mhuire, a Mháthair Dé, guigh orainn na peacaigh, anois agus ar uair ár mbáis.
Amen.

Solemnity of the Assumption of the Blessed Virgin Mary,
Knock, August 2013

CONTENTS

Foreword   xvii

SECTION ONE
FAMILIAR PRAYERS

Sign of the Cross   3
Comhartha na Croise   3
A Morning Offering Prayer   3
Our Father   4
An Phaidir   4
Hail Mary   5
Sé do Bheatha, a Mhuire   5
Glory be to the Father   6
Glóir don Athair   6
The Angelus   7
Regina Coeli   8
Prayer to Guardian Angel   8
Memorare   9
Hail Holy Queen   9
Grace Before Meals   10
Grace After Meals   10
Acts of Contrition   11
Nicene Creed   12
Apostles' Creed   14
Agnus Dei   15
Saint Patrick's Breastplate   15
Make Me an Instrument of Your Peace   16
Christ Has No Body   17
The Beatitudes   18

Eternal Rest   19

Prayer to the Holy Spirit   19

The Divine Praises   20

Prayer to St Joseph   21

St Joseph, Loving Father   22

To My Patron Saint   23

Trusting in Your Providence   24

The Mysteries of the Rosary   25

Traditional Stations of the Cross   29

SECTION TWO
CHILDREN'S PRAYERS

Act of Sorrow   41

An Gníomh Dóláis   41

A Child's Prayer for Parents and Family   42

A Child's Prayer for Parents   42

A Child's Prayer for their Father   43

A Child's Prayer for their Mother   43

A Prayer for Mum and Dad   44

A Child's Prayer for Brothers and Sisters   45

Thanks for My Grandparents   46

Thanks for My Family   47

Prayer for Forgiveness   48

Paidir ag iarraidh Maithiúnais   48

Prayer After Forgiveness   49

Paidir tar éis Maithiúnais   49

Grace Before Meals   50

Altú roimh Bhia   50

Grace After Meals   51

Altú tar éis Bhia   51

God, our Creator   52
Journey Prayer   53
Paidir Thurais   53
Morning Prayer   54
Paidir na Maidine   54
A Child's Prayer for Morning   54
Night Prayer   55
Paidir na hOíche   55
A Child's Prayer for Evening   56
A Child's Evening Hymn   56
A Child's Prayer of Praise   57
A Child's Prayer for Pets   57
A Child's Prayer for School   58
A Child's Prayer of Thanksgiving   59
Prayer to the Trinity   59
Paidir don Tríonóid Naofa   59
'Let's Pray' Prayers from *Alive-O*   60
'Pray Together' Prayers from *Alive-O*   62

SECTION THREE
FAMILY PRAYERS FOR ALL OCCASIONS

Prayers for an Engaged Couple   67
Prayer of the Newly Married Couple   70
For Newlyweds   71
Prayers for Married Couples   72
In Support of Couples   74
For All Married Couples   76
For Couples   77
Litany of Blessing   78
Bless This House   79

Hospitality   80
For a Married Couple Before
   Becoming Parents   81
Choose Life: Prayer for the Child
   in the Womb   82
Prayer from *Evangelium Vitae*   83
For a Newborn   84
For Our Children   84
Children's First Experience of the
   Family of the Church   85
Children, the Precious Gift of Marriage   85
The Broader Communion of the Family   86
For Children (by Parents)   86
Mother's Day   87
Father's Day   87
Fathers and Mothers   88
A Husband's Prayer   89
A Wife's Prayer   89
Universal Prayer for Grandparents   90
An Elderly Person   91
A Prayer for Irish Emigrants   92
A Prayer for Immigrants   93
A Birthday Blessing   94
Birthday Prayers   95
Wedding Anniversary   96
Silver Wedding Anniversary   96
Golden Wedding Anniversary   97
Wedding Anniversary   98
Prayer to St Valentine   99
A Valentine Prayer   100
Changes On Our Journey   101
Blessing Upon Retirement   102

God's Plan for Our Marriage
   and Family   104
Living in Justice and in Love   105
General Blessing for a Family
   or Household   106
Blessing for a Family and their Home   107
For Families   108
Family Times and Moments of Friendship   109
The Family   110
Prayers for Families   111
A Family Prayer   112

SECTION FOUR
IN TIMES OF NEED AND DIFFICULTY

Jesus, You Are With Me   117
For Parents of a Sick Child   118
For One Ill in Hospital   119
Parents Who Have Suffered a Miscarriage   120
For Carers   121
A Prayer for a Family Affected
   by Addiction   122
Prayer For Students Taking Exams   123
Missing Persons   124
Lend Me Your Hand   125
Prayer to Our Lady   126
A Prayer at Night (Psalm 4)   127
Be Like the Good Samaritan   128
Prayer in Time of Pain or Difficulty   129
Prayer with the Dying   130
For a Widow or Widower   131

The Recently Bereaved   132
Prayer for the Dead   133
We Give Them Back to Thee, O God   134
For a Father Who Has Died   135
For a Mother Who Has Died   135
In Remembrance   136
On the Loss of a Husband or Wife   137

SECTION FIVE
SEASONS, VALUES AND REFLECTIONS

Advent   141
Advent Wreath   142
Advent Prayer   143
Jesse Tree   144
Christmas Crib Prayers   145
Christmas   147
Blessing of the New Year;
   Be With Us, Lord   148
New Year Prayer   149
Daily Lenten Prayer   150
Lent   151
Easter Prayer   152
Easter   153
Autumn   154
Winter   155
Spring   156
Summer   157
The Seasons of Our Love   158
The Church is a Home for Everyone   159
Living Our Values   159

The Difference Between
   'Having' and 'Being'   160
The Gift of Every Life from God   161
Praise for the Gift of Life   162
Be a Sign and Presence of the
   Love of Jesus   163
Prayer for Marriage and the Family   164
With a Love of Preference for the
   Most Disadvantaged   165
For World Peace   166
For Peace   167
Prayers for Those Caring for the Aged   168
Litany for a Growth in Love   170
50th International
   Eucharistic Congress Prayer   171
The Call of the Bell   172
God's Love Has Been Given to Us   173
We are Prophets of a Future
   Not Our Own   174
A Creed to Live By   175
God in an Apron   177
Through the Year   179

APPENDIX ONE
GOD'S WORD AND MARRIAGE AND FAMILY

   Marriage   183
   Parenting   185
   Family and Friends   187

APPENDIX TWO
PRAYERS FROM THE CELEBRATION OF MARRIAGE

Nuptial Blessing (1)   191
Nuptial Blessing (2)   194
Nuptial Blessing (3)   196
Solemn Blessing from the Celebration
    of Marriage   198
Collects from the Celebration of Marriage   199
Cross of St Brigid Blessing   200
Beannacht ag Deireach an Aifrinn   201

Acknowledgements   203

FOREWORD

This prayer book comes from a dream, an encouragement and a journey to create and compile something special. Treat it as your own. This prayer book is yours.

Saint Teresa of Ávila experienced prayer as an intimate sharing between friends, involving taking time frequently to be with God, who we know loves us.

Sometimes in different situations and experiences, we find ourselves searching for a prayer that helps us to respond to experiences, occasions, challenges and joys on the journey of life.

This prayer book can be used by those preparing for marriage and in married life, by family members and families, for personal prayer and prayer together. It offers prayers for daily use or it can be dipped into from time to time, using the section and prayer titles to guide you towards your choice.

This prayer book invites you to bring the hopes and concerns in your marriage and the needs of your family to God as you listen to him, to pause and take time to know Jesus better, to praise and thank God, and to pray for the needs of the community transformed by marriage and family life.

In the words of Pope Francis,
'Prayer, humility and charity towards all are essential in the Christian life: they are the way to holiness.'

May God be with you always.
Dia anseo isteach.

SECTION ONE

FAMILIAR PRAYERS

Sign of the Cross

In the name of the Father, and of the Son,
and of the Holy Spirit. Amen.

Comhartha na Croise

In ainm an Athar, agus an Mhic,
agus an Spioraid Naoimh. Áiméan.

A Morning Offering Prayer

O Jesus, through the most pure heart of Mary,
I offer you all my thoughts, words and actions,
prayers, pains and sufferings of this day
for all the intentions of thy Divine Heart,
so that at the end of the day I may be able to say
I have tried to love you more, love others and love
myself more.
I make this prayer through Christ, Our Lord.
Amen.

Our Father

> Our Father, who art in heaven,
> Hallowed be thy name;
> thy kingdom come,
> thy will be done
> on earth as it is in heaven.
> Give us this day our daily bread
> and forgive us our trespasses,
> as we forgive those who trespass against us;
> and lead us not into temptation,
> But deliver us from evil. Amen.

An Phaidir

> Ár nAthair, atá ar neamh,
> go naofar d'ainm,
> go dtaga do ríocht,
> go ndéantar do thoil ar an talamh
> mar a dhéantar ar neamh.
> Ár n-arán laethúil tabhair dúinn inniu,
> agus maith dúinn ár bhfiacha,
> mar a mhaithimidne dár bhféichiúna féin,
> agus ná lig sinn i gcathú,
> ach saor sinn ó olc. Áiméan.

Hail Mary

Hail Mary, full of grace,
The Lord is with thee.
Blessed art thou among women
And blessed is the fruit of thy womb, Jesus.
Holy Mary, mother of God,
Pray for us sinners,
Now, and at the hour of our death. Amen.

Sé do Bheatha, a Mhuire

Sé do bheatha, a Mhuire,
Atá lán de ghrásta,
Tá an Tiarna leat.
Is beannaithe thú idir mhná,
Agus is beannaithe toradh do bhroinne, Íosa.
A Naomh Mhuire, a mháthair Dé,
Guigh orainn, na peacaigh,
Anois agus ar uair ár mbáis. Áiméan.

Glory be to the Father
>Glory be to the Father,
And to the Son,
And to the Holy Spirit;
As it was in the beginning,
Is now and ever shall be,
World without end. Amen.

Glóir don Athair
>Glóir don Athair,
Agus don Mhac,
Agus don Spiorad Naomh.
Mar a bhí ó thús,
Mar atá anois,
Mar a bheas go brách,
Le saol na saol. Áiméan.

The Angelus

The angel of the Lord declared unto Mary
And she conceived by the Holy Spirit.
Hail Mary …

Behold the handmaid of the Lord
Be it done unto me according to thy word.
Hail Mary …

And the Word was made flesh
And dwelt among us.
Hail Mary …

Pray for us, O holy Mother of God,
That we may be made worthy of the promises of
Christ.

Let us pray.
Pour forth, we beseech you, O Lord, your grace
into our hearts, that we, to whom the Incarnation
of Christ, your Son, was made known by the
message of an angel may by his passion and cross
be brought to the glory of his resurrection,
through the same Christ our Lord.
Amen.

Regina Coeli

Queen of Heaven, rejoice. Alleluia.
For he, whom you were worthy to bear, Alleluia,
Has risen, as he promised. Alleluia.
Pray for us to God. Alleluia.
Rejoice and be glad, O Virgin Mary, Alleluia,
Because the Lord has truly risen. Alleluia.

Let us pray:
O God, who gladdened the world by the
resurrection of your Son, our Lord Jesus Christ;
grant, we pray, that through the Virgin Mary, his
mother, we may enter into the joys of eternal life.
Through the same Christ our Lord. Amen.

Prayer to Guardian Angel

Oh Angel of God, my Guardian dear
to whom God's love commits me here.
Ever this day be at my side
to light and guard to rule and guide.
Amen.

Memorare

Remember, O most gracious Virgin Mary,
that never was it known
that anyone who fled to thy protection,
implored thy help,
or sought thine intercession was left unaided.
Inspired by this confidence, I fly unto thee,
O Virgin of virgins, my mother;
to thee do I come, before thee I stand, sinful and
sorrowful.
O Mother of the Word Incarnate,
despise not my petitions,
but in thy mercy hear and answer me. Amen.

❖ ❖ ❖

Hail Holy Queen

Hail, holy Queen, mother of mercy;
Hail our life, our sweetness, and our hope!
To you we cry, poor banished children of Eve;
To you we send up our sighs, mourning and
weeping
in this valley of tears.
Turn then, most gracious advocate,
Your eyes of mercy towards us;
And after this our exile,
Show to us the blessed fruit of your womb, Jesus.
O clement, O loving, O sweet Virgin Mary.
Pray for us, O holy Mother of God,
That we may be made worthy of the promises of
Christ.

❖ ❖ ❖

Grace Before Meals

Bless us, O Lord, and these, thy gifts,
which we are about to receive from thy bounty.
Through Christ, our Lord. Amen.

Grace After Meals

We give thee thanks for all your benefits, O
Almighty God, who livest and reignest world
without end. Amen.
May the souls of the faithful departed, through
the mercy of God, rest in peace. Amen.

Acts of Contrition

O my God, I am heartily sorry
for having offended you
and I detest my sins
above every other evil
because they displease you, my God,
Who, in your infinite wisdom,
are so deserving of all my love
and I firmly resolve
with the help of your grace
never more to offend you
and to amend my life.
Amen.

O my God, I am heartily sorry
for all my sins because they
offend you who are infinitely good.
And I firmly resolve
with the help of your grace
never to offend you again. Amen.

Nicene Creed

I believe in one God,
the Father almighty,
maker of heaven and earth,
of all things visible and invisible.

I believe in one Lord Jesus Christ,
the Only Begotten Son of God,
born of the Father before all ages.
God from God, Light from Light,
true God from true God,
begotten, not made, consubstantial with the
Father;
through him all things were made.
For us men and for our salvation
he came down from heaven,
and by the Holy Spirit was incarnate of the Virgin
Mary,
and became man.

For our sake he was crucified under Pontius
Pilate,
he suffered death and was buried,
and rose again on the third day
in accordance with the Scriptures.
He ascended into heaven
and is seated at the right hand of the Father.

He will come again in glory
to judge the living and the dead
and his kingdom will have no end.

I believe in the Holy Spirit, the Lord, the giver of
life,
who proceeds from the Father and the Son,
who with the Father and the Son is adored and
glorified,
who has spoken through the prophets.

I believe in one, holy, catholic and apostolic
Church.
I confess one Baptism for the forgiveness of sins
and I look forward to the resurrection of the dead
and the life of the world to come. Amen.

Apostles' Creed

I believe in God,
the Father almighty,
Creator of heaven and earth,
and in Jesus Christ, his only Son, our Lord,
who was conceived by the Holy Spirit,
born of the Virgin Mary,
suffered under Pontius Pilate,
was crucified, died and was buried;
he descended into hell;
on the third day he rose again from the dead;
he ascended into heaven,
and is seated at the right hand of God the Father
almighty;
from there he will come to judge the living and
the dead.

I believe in the Holy Spirit,
the holy catholic Church,
the communion of saints,
the forgiveness of sins,
the resurrection of the body,
and life everlasting. Amen.

Agnus Dei

    Lamb of God, you take away the sins of the
world, have mercy on us.
Lamb of God, you take away the sins of the
world, have mercy on us.
Lamb of God, you take away the sins of the
world, grant us peace.

Saint Patrick's Breastplate

    Christ with me, Christ before me,
Christ behind me, Christ within me,
Christ beneath me, Christ above me,
Christ at my right, Christ at my left.

Christ in the heart of everyone who
thinks of me,
Christ in the mouth of everyone
who speaks of me,
Christ in every eye that sees me,
Christ in every ear that hears me.

I bind to myself today
the strong name
of the Trinity.

Make Me an Instrument of Your Peace

Lord, make me an instrument of your peace.
Where there is hatred, let me sow love;
where there is injury, pardon;
where there is doubt, faith;
where there is despair, hope;
where there is darkness, light;
and where there is sadness, joy.

O Divine Master, grant that I may not so much seek
to be consoled as to console;
to be understood as to understand;
to be loved as to love.
For it is in giving that we receive;
it is in pardoning that we are pardoned;
and it is in dying that we are born to eternal life.
Amen.

Inspired by the spirituality of St Francis of Assisi

Christ Has No Body

Christ has no body but yours,
No hands, no feet on earth but yours,
Yours are the eyes with which he looks
Compassion on this world.
Yours are the feet with which he walks to do
good,
Yours are the hands, with which he blesses all the
world.
Ours are the hands, yours are the feet,
Yours are the eyes, you are his body.
Christ has no body now but yours,
No hands, no feet on earth but yours,
Yours are the eyes with which he looks
Compassion on this world,
Christ has no body now on earth but yours.

Often attributed to the inspiration of the
spirituality of St Teresa of Ávila

The Beatitudes

Blessed are the poor in spirit,
for theirs is the kingdom of heaven.
Blessed are those who mourn,
for they will be comforted.
Blessed are the meek,
for they will inherit the earth.
Blessed are those who hunger and thirst
for righteousness, for they will be filled.
Blessed are the merciful,
for they will receive mercy.
Blessed are the pure in heart,
for they will see God.
Blessed are the peacemakers,
for they will be called children of God.
Blessed are those who are persecuted for
righteousness' sake,
for theirs is the kingdom of heaven.

Blessed are you when people revile you and
persecute you and utter all kinds of evil against
you falsely on my account.
Rejoice and be glad, for your reward is great in
heaven, for in the same way they persecuted the
prophets who were before you.

(Cf. Mt 5:1-12, Lk 6:20-22), *Alive-O 7*

Eternal Rest

Eternal rest grant unto them, O Lord,
and let perpetual light shine upon them.
May their souls and the souls of the faithful
departed,
through the mercy of God, rest in peace. Amen.

Prayer to the Holy Spirit

Come Holy Spirit, fill the hearts of your faithful
and kindle in them the fire of your love.
Send forth your Spirit and they shall be created,
And you shall renew the face of the earth.

The Divine Praises

Blessed be God.

Blessed be his holy name.

Blessed be Jesus Christ, true God and true man.

Blessed be the name of Jesus.

Blessed be his most Sacred Heart.

Blessed be his most precious Blood.

Blessed be Jesus in the most Holy Sacrament of the altar.

Blessed be the Holy Spirit, the Paraclete.

Blessed be the great Mother of God, Mary most holy.

Blessed be her holy and Immaculate Conception.

Blessed be her glorious Assumption.

Blessed be the name of Mary, Virgin and mother.

Blessed be St Joseph, her most chaste spouse.

Blessed be God in his angels and in his saints.

Prayer to St Joseph

O glorious St Joseph,
You who have power to render possible
even things that are considered impossible,
come to our aid in our present
trouble and distress.
Take this important and difficult
affair under your particular
protection, that it may end happily.

O dear St Joseph, all our confidence
is in you.
Let it not be said that we would
Invoke you in vain; and since you are so powerful
with Jesus and Mary, show that your goodness
equals your power.
Amen.

St Joseph, Loving Father
> Saint Joseph,
> Obtain for us the spirit of wisdom,
> That it may guide us in all our ways,
> In our interior and exterior life.
> Care for us, like a loving father,
> In all our concerns,
> Both temporal and eternal,
> And especially on this present day,
> And for a good death when we die.
> Amen.

YOUCAT: Youth Prayer Book, p. 137

To My Patron Saint (I bear your name)
Dear Saint (name),
Ever since my baptism, I bear your name.
Pray for me to God –
For the strength of your faith,
The breadth of your hope,
The courage of your love.
Support me so that I, like you,
May hear God's loving call today,
And in my life may answer
As God's grace moves me to.
Then one day, with you and all the saints,
May I receive the crown of life.
Amen.

YOUCAT: Youth Prayer Book, p. 137

Trusting in Your Providence
>   O Lord, you have told us
>   that our Father in heaven will care for us,
>   just as he cares for the lilies of the field
>   and the birds of heaven.
>   You, who did not even have a place
>   to lay your weary head,
>   be our teacher.
>
>   Teach us to trust in God's providence,
>   and help us to overcome our human greed.
>   For greed never made anyone happy.
>
>   Give us the strength to give ourselves totally to
>   you,
>   and so be an instrument
>   to fulfil your will.
>
>   Bless the use of money in the world,
>   so that the hungry may be fed,
>   the naked clothed, the poor sheltered,
>   and the sick cared for.
>
>   And grant us, Lord, your Holy Spirit,
>   so that we may clearly recognise,
>   through the faith you grant us,
>   that we are all worth more in your sight
>   than any beautiful lily
>   or any singing skylark in the air.
>   Amen.

Blessed Teresa of Calcutta,
YOUCAT: Youth Prayer Book, p. 144

❖ ❖ ❖

The Mysteries of the Rosary
The Joyful Mysteries (Monday & Saturday)
First Mystery: The Annunciation of Our Lord
Rejoice, you who enjoy God's favour!

Lk 1:26-38

Second Mystery: The Visitation
Of all women you are the most blessed, and
blessed is the fruit of your womb.

Lk 1:40-42

Third Mystery: The Birth of Jesus
And she gave birth to a son, her first born.

Lk 2:1-20

Fourth Mystery: The Presentation of Our Lord
They took him up to Jerusalem to present him to
the Lord.

Lk 2:22-38

Fifth Mystery: The Finding of Jesus in the Temple
They found him in the Temple, sitting among the
teachers.

Lk 2:41-50

The Sorrowful Mysteries (Tuesday & Friday)

First Mystery: The Agony in the Garden
But let it be as you, not I, would have it.

Mk 14:32-42

Second Mystery: The Scourging at the Pillar
After having Jesus scourged he handed him over
to be crucified.

Mt 27:11-26

Third Mystery: The Crowning with Thorns
And having twisted some thorns into a crown
they put this on his head.

Mt 27:27-31

Fourth Mystery: The Carrying of the Cross
They seized on a man, Simon from Cyrene, who
was coming in from the country, and made him
shoulder the cross and carry it behind Jesus.

Lk 23:26-32

Fifth Mystery: The Crucifixion
It was the third hour when they crucified him.

Mk 15:23-29

❖ ❖ ❖

The Glorious Mysteries (Wednesday & Sunday)

First Mystery: The Resurrection
He is not here; he has risen.

Lk 24:1-6

Second Mystery: The Ascension
As he said this he was lifted up as they looked on,
and a cloud took him from their sight.

Acts 1:6-11

Third Mystery: The Descent of the Holy Spirit
They were all filled with the Holy Spirit and
began to speak.

Acts 2:1-4

Fourth Mystery: The Assumption of Mary
I shall return to take you to myself.

Jn 14:1-3

Fifth Mystery: The Crowning of Mary
And on her head a crown of twelve stars.

Rev 12:1-17

The Mysteries of Light (Thursday)
First Mystery: The Baptism in the Jordan
This is my Son, the Beloved; my favour rests on him.

Mt 3:13-17

Second Mystery: The Manifestation of Jesus at Cana
His mother said to the servants, 'Do whatever he tells you.'

Jn 2:1-12

Third Mystery: The Proclamation of the Kingdom
The time is fulfilled, and the kingdom of God is close at hand.

Mk 1:14-15

Fourth Mystery: The Transfiguration on Mount Tabor
There in their presence he was transfigured.

Mk 9:2-7

Fifth Mystery: The Institution of the Eucharist
This is my body given for you.

Lk 22:14-20

Scripture references from the Jerusalem Bible

Traditional Stations of the Cross

Before each Station
Leader: We adore you, O Christ, and we bless you.
Response: Because by your Holy Cross you have redeemed the world.

After each Station
Response: Lord Jesus, help us walk in your steps.

First Station: Jesus is condemned to death
The Words of Christ
'Watch out for yourselves. They will hand you over to the courts. You will be beaten in synagogues. You will be arraigned before governors and kings because of me, as a witness before them.'

Mk 13:9

Prayer
Leader: Lord, give us strength to stand as a witness and praise your name through all struggles and condemnation. May we rejoice as we follow you even to death and share in the hope of your everlasting Kingdom.
R: Amen.

Second Station: Jesus takes up his cross
The Words of Christ
'Whoever wishes to come after me must deny himself, take up his cross, and follow me.'

Mt 16:24

Prayer
Leader: Lord, grant us humility as we stand before your Cross, burdened by the weight of our sins. May we faithfully follow you for you are the way, the truth and the life that leads us to everlasting freedom.
R: Amen.

Third Station: Jesus falls the first time
The Words of Christ
'Father, if you are willing, take this cup away from me; still, not my will but yours be done.'

Lk 22:42

Prayer
Leader: Lord open our hearts that we might graciously accept your will for us. May we not be discouraged or distracted by words and actions that seek to harm us as we travel along your way to the Kingdom.
R: Amen.

Fourth Station: Jesus meets his mother

The Words of Christ
'Woman, behold, your son.'

Jn 19:26

Prayer
Leader: Lord like your Blessed Mother, may we be
faithful to your command to follow you so that at
the end of time we may join the lowly in
proclaiming your glory.
R: Amen.

Fifth Station: Simon of Cyrene helps Jesus

The Words of Christ
'You know that the rulers of the Gentiles lord it
over them, and the great ones make their
authority over them felt. But it shall not be so
among you. Rather, whoever wishes to be great
among you shall be your servant.'

Mt 25-26

Prayer
Leader: Lord, you are the Creator and author of
all things. You show us the strength of the weak,
the greatness of the servant. Give us prayerful
hands and supple knees that we might bend easily
to your will and serve those whom you love.
R: Amen.

Sixth Station: Veronica wipes the face of Jesus
The Words of Christ
'Courage, daughter! Your faith has saved you.'

Mt 9:22

'You are the light of the world … Your light must shine before others, that they may see your good deeds and glorify your heavenly Father.'

Mt 5:14, 16

Prayer
Leader: Give us faith, that we might pursue you with loving and dedicated hearts. Give us courage, that we may stand before others and reflect your presence in the world.
R: Amen.

Seventh Station: Jesus falls a second time
The Words of Christ
'Blessed are you when they insult you and persecute you and utter every kind of evil against you (falsely) because of me.'

Mt 5:11

Prayer
Leader: Lord, grant us the strength and courage to rise again each time we fall and to seek your mercy in compassion.
R: Amen.

Eighth Station: Jesus speaks to the women of Jerusalem

The Words of Christ

'Daughters of Jerusalem, do not weep for me; weep instead for yourselves and for your children, for indeed, the days are coming when people will say, 'Blessed are the barren, the wombs that never bore and the breasts that never nursed.' At that time people will say to the mountains, 'Fall upon us!' and to the hills, 'Cover us!' for if these things are done when the wood is green what will happen when it is dry?'

Lk 23:28-31

Prayer

Leader: Lord, turn our cries of mourning for what we have lost to songs of joy for we have found you who opened the gates to God's heavenly Kingdom.
R: Amen.

Ninth Station: Jesus falls the third time

The Words of Christ

'When they lead you away and hand you over, do not worry beforehand about what you are to say. But say whatever will be given to you at that hour. For it will not be you who are speaking but the Holy Spirit.'

Mk 13:11

Prayer

Lord, put your name on our lips that we may rely on you for help to remain steadfast in times of struggle.
R: Amen.

Tenth Station: Jesus is stripped of his clothes
The Words of Christ
'Bless those who curse you, pray for those who
mistreat you. To the person who strikes you on
one cheek, offer the other one as well, and from
the person who takes your cloak, do not withhold
even your tunic.'

Lk 6:28-29

Prayer
Leader: Lord, may we be clothed only in your
truth as we walk among the faithless and may we
be freed from the desires that lead us away from
you.
R: Amen.

Eleventh Station: Jesus is nailed to the cross
The Words of Christ
'Father, forgive them, they know not what they do.'

Lk 23:34

Prayer
Leader: Lord, for our sake you were nailed to a
Cross and given over as a Sacrifice for our sins. In
gratitude may we boldly embrace your Cross and
live in the love that you poured out to save us.
R: Amen.

Twelfth Station: Jesus dies on the cross
The Words of Christ
'Eloi, Eloi, lama sabachthani? … My God, My
God, why have you forsaken me?'

Mk 15:33-34, 37

'Amen, I say to you, today you will be with me in
Paradise'

Lk 23:43

Prayer
Leader: Lord, you did not forsake us when we
disobeyed your Word, but sent your only Son as a
sign of your love for us. May his sacrifice on the
cross lead us to love others and seek the good of
your Kingdom.
R: Amen.

**Thirteenth Station: Jesus is removed from the
cross**
The Words of Christ
'The hour has come for the Son of Man to be
glorified. Amen, amen, I say to you, unless a grain
of wheat falls to the ground and dies, it remains
just a grain of wheat; but if it dies, it produces
much fruit.'

Jn 23-24

Prayer
Leader: Lord, may our bodies always be one with
the Body of Christ broken and shared for others
so that all might live in the new life of your
resurrection.
R: Amen.

Fourteenth Station: Jesus is placed in the Tomb
The Words of Christ
'This is my commandment: love one another as I
love you. No one has greater love than this, to lay
down one's life for one's friends.'

Jn 15:12-13

Prayer
Leader: Lord, your love for us exceeds all bounds.
Even death cannot separate us from your love.
May we share the love that knows no end with all
who seek you.
R: Amen.

Fifteenth Station: Resurrection of Jesus
The Words of Christ
'All power in heaven and on earth has been given
to me. Go, therefore, and make disciples of all
nations, baptising them in the name of the
Father, and of the Son, and of the Holy Spirit,
teaching them to observe all that I have
commanded you. And behold, I am with you
always, until the end of the age.'

Mt 28:18-20

Prayer
All: Blessed are the poor in spirit, for theirs is the
kingdom of heaven.
Blessed are those who mourn, for they will be
comforted.
Blessed are the meek, for they will inherit the
land.

Blessed are they who hunger and thirst for righteousness, for they will be satisfied.
Blessed are the merciful, for they will be shown mercy.
Blessed are the clean of heart, for they will see God.
Blessed are the peacemakers, for they will be called children of God.
Blessed are they who are persecuted for the sake of righteousness,
For theirs is the kingdom of Heaven.

Mt 5:3-10

Closing Prayer
Leader: Lord Jesus Christ, your passion and death is the sacrifice that unites earth and heaven and reconciles all people to you. May we who have faithfully reflected on these mysteries follow in your steps and so come to share your glory in heaven where you live and reign with the Father and the Holy Spirit, one God, forever and ever.
R: Amen.

Catholic Household Blessings and Prayers, pp. 446–5

SECTION TWO

CHILDREN'S PRAYERS

Act of Sorrow

O my God, I thank you for loving me.
I am sorry for all my sins, for not loving
others and not loving you.
Help me to live like Jesus and not sin again.
Amen.

An Gníomh Dóláis

A Dhia, gabhaim buíochas leat as ucht do ghrá
dom.
Tá brón orm faoi mo pheacaí uile:
Nach raibh grá agam duitse ná do dhaoine eile.
Cabhraigh liom mo shaol a chaitheamh ar nós
Íosa
Agus gan peaca a dhéanamh arís. Áiméan.

A Child's Prayer for Parents and Family

O God, bless our home, our family, friends and neighbours; and give us thankful hearts for all your mercies. Amen.

Dear God, I am glad that you love daddy and mammy and me and everybody. I want to love You, too, and to grow up to be strong and good. Bless us today and keep us in your care. Dear Father in heaven, I thank you for Jesus who came to bring us your love, and to teach us to love one another; for Mary who carried your Son; for Joseph who protected them both in the Holy Family. Help our family to be made perfect in their example. Amen.

A Child's Prayer for Parents

Heavenly Father, I thank you for my father and mother and for our home. Bless us all and help us to love you and in love to serve one another as Jesus taught us to do. Give me strength to do what is right today and to do for others what I would want them to do for me. Amen.

A Child's Prayer for their Father

I thank you, Lord, for my father. Grant me to realise the depth of his love for me so often left unspoken, and to appreciate his great and continuous sacrifices.

His fatherly care reflects your divine care; his strength, your power; his understanding, your wisdom. He is your faithful servant and image.

Bless him with peace of soul, health of body and success in his life. Amen.

Stephen Cummins

A Child's Prayer for their Mother

I thank you, Lord, for my mother. Let me never forget the depth of her love
for me and to appreciate her many and continuous sacrifices.

Her motherly care reflects your divine care; her strength, your power; her understanding, your wisdom.

Bless her Lord with peace of soul, health of mind and body and be for her
a source of strength and support. Amen.

Stephen Cummins

A Prayer for Mum and Dad
>Lord Jesus,
>in your relationship with Mary and Joseph,
>you were a model of respect and obedience
>and of love toward your parents.
>
>I need your help.
>
>Help me always to show true gratitude
>for all that my parents have done for me.
>
>Give them health and long life.
>Bless their works and plans,
>help them in their own difficulties.
>
>Help me to dialogue with them
>and to accept them with their strengths and their
>weaknesses.
>
>Help them to understand me with the same
>patience,
>So that together we might be able
>to overcome moments of misunderstanding and
>incomprehension.
>
>I ask you Lord,
>that in our family,
>love, peace and joy will live always
>as in your family of Nazareth.

Rev Peter Murphy

❖ ❖ ❖

A Child's Prayer for Brothers and Sisters

Dear Lord, I thank you for my brothers and sisters. Though sometimes we quarrel and bicker, help us to be more patient. Help us to know when teasing is fun and when it begins to hurt and annoy; help us never to be jealous of those older ones who have privileges we do not. Give us patience with those younger and weaker and more in need of our care and concern. Teach us to share cheerfully; not to tattle; to be understanding. Give to me and all of us the gifts of strong loyalty and deep love for our family. Amen.

Prayerbook: A Catholic Religious Site

Thanks for My Grandparents

Lord of life,
Thank you for the gift of my grandparents.

Thank you because they are near to me,
they encourage me to give my best
and with their wisdom
they often give me the gems of wisdom
that only come with years.

Thank you for their important role
in our daily family life.

I am grateful for the way they can listen to my
problems and worries.

I am grateful for the way they share with me,
through their example,
the most important values in life.

Lord, grant them the gift of serenity as they grow
older,
I pray that I may never lack their thoughtfulness
and faith. Amen.

Rev Peter Murphy

Thanks for My Family

Lord Jesus,
You also needed a mother and a father to grow.
Thanks for my parents.
What would my life be without them?
Help me to be always grateful for
the gift which they are to me.

Rev Peter Murphy

Prayer for Forgiveness

O my God, help me to remember the times when
I didn't live as Jesus asked me to.
Help me to be sorry and to try again. Amen.

Paidir ag iarraidh Maithiúnais

A Dhia, ár nAthair, cabhraigh liom cuimhneamh
ar na huaireanta nár mhair mé mar a d'iarr Íosa
orm.
Cabhraigh liom brón a bheith orm
agus iarracht eile a dhéanamh. Áiméan.

Alive-O/Beo go Deo

Prayer After Forgiveness
> O my God, thank you for forgiving me.
> Help me to love others.
> Help me to live as Jesus asked me to. Amen.

Paidir tar éis Maithiúnais
> A Dhia, ár nAthair, go raibh maith agat faoi
> mhaithiúnas a thabhairt dom.
> Cabhraigh liom grá a thabhairt do dhaoine eile.
> Cabhraigh liom maireachtáil mar a d'iarr Íosa
> orm. Áiméan.

Alive-O/Beo go Deo

Grace Before Meals

Bless us, O God, as we sit together.
Bless the food we eat today.
Bless the hands that made the food.
Bless us, O God. Amen.

Altú roimh Bhia

Beannacht ó Dhia orainne atá ag suí chun boird
le chéile.
Beannacht ar an mbia a ithimid inniu.
Beannacht ar na lámha a d'ullmhaigh dúinn é.
Beannacht, a Dhia dhílis, orainn féin. Áiméan.

Alive-O/Beo go Deo

Grace After Meals
> Thank you, God, for the food we have eaten.
> Thank you, God, for all our friends.
> Thank you, God, for everything.
> Thank you, God. Amen.

Altú tar éis Bhia
> Go raibh maith agat, a Dhia, mar is tú a thug bia
> dúinn.
> Go raibh maith agat, a Dhia, mar is tú a thug
> cairde dúinn.
> Go raibh maith agat, a Dhia, mar is tú a thug
> gach rud dúinn.
> Go raibh maith agat, a Dhia. Áiméan.

Alive-O/Beo go Deo

God, our Creator

> God, Our Creator,
> We thank you for giving us your time.
> Time to run, time to walk,
> Time to start, time to stop,
> Time to drink, time to eat,
> Time to wake, time to sleep,
> Time to laugh, time to cry,
> Time for hello, time for goodbye,
> Time to work, time to play,
> Time to watch, time to pray.
> Thank you, God, for your time every day.
> Amen.

Alive-O

Journey Prayer
> Arise with me in the morning,
> Travel with me through each day,
> Welcome me on my arrival.
> God, be with me all the way. Amen.

Paidir Thurais
> Éirigh liom, a Dhia,
> Fan liom i rith an lae,
> Sa bhaile agus ar gach turas,
> Ná lig dom dul ar strae. Áiméan.

Alive-O/Beo go Deo

Morning Prayer

Father in heaven, you love me,
You're with me night and day.
I want to love you always
In all I do and say.
I'll try to please you, Father.
Bless me through the day. Amen.

Paidir na Maidine

A Dhia, tá grá agat dom.
Bíonn tú liom de lá is d'oíche
Ba mhaith liom grá a thabhairt duit
Gach nóiméad den lá.
Ba mhaith liom tú a shásamh.
A Athair, cabhraigh liom. Áiméan.

Alive-O/Beo go Deo

❖ ❖ ❖

A Child's Prayer for Morning

My God, I offer to you this day all I think and do
and say, in union with all you have done for me
by Jesus Christ your Son. Amen.

Dear Lord, I rise from bed to pray: then soon go
out to school or play. Let all I meet along the way
see you in me throughout the day. Amen.

Prayerbook: A Catholic Religious Site

❖ ❖ ❖

Night Prayer

God, our Father, I come to say
Thank you for your love today.
Thank you for my family,
And all the friends you give to me.
Guard me in the dark of night,
And in the morning send your light. Amen.

Paidir na hOíche

A Dhia, a Athair, molaim thú
As ucht do chineáltais liom inniu.
As ucht mo chairde molaim thú,
Agus as an teaghlach a thug tú dom.
I ndorchadas na hoíche cosain mé;
Solas na maidine go bhfeice mé. Áiméan.

Alive-O/Beo go Deo

A Child's Prayer for Evening

Lord, keep us safe this night, safe from all our
earthly fears; may angels guard us while we sleep,
till morning comes and light appears. Amen.

Now I lay me down to sleep; I pray you, Lord,
my life to keep. If I should die before I wake, I
pray the Lord my soul to take. Amen.

Prayerbook: A Catholic Religious Site

A Child's Evening Hymn

I hear no voice, I feel no touch,
I see no glory bright;
But yet I know that God is near,
in darkness as in light.

He watches ever by my side
And hears my whispered prayer;
The Father for his little child
Both night and day does care.

Catholic Household Blessings and Prayers, p. 63

A Child's Prayer of Praise

Dear Jesus, I love you. Please help me each day to be kind, to be gentle, and to obey quickly. Amen.

Two little eyes to look at God. Two little ears to hear his word. Two little lips to sing his praise. Two little feet to walk his ways. Two little hands to do his will. One little heart to love him still. Amen.

Prayerbook: A Catholic Religious Site

A Child's Prayer for Pets

O Lord, you let animals be near you at your birth. Teach us to be kind and gentle to all animals; may we always care and provide for our pets, and never ill-treat any living creature that you have put upon earth. Amen.

Prayerbook: A Catholic Religious Site

A Child's Prayer for School

Dear God, come with me to school, be with me
in my lessons and in my play. Help me to be
friendly and thoughtful, obedient to my teachers,
careful in my studies and like Jesus in my words
and deeds. Amen.

Come, Holy Spirit, and help me in my lessons.
Open my eyes and ears to your world about me;
the sun and stars and space, numbers and letters
and words, people and places and ideas. Give me
the will to listen and learn; the patience to work
well; the courage to seek and to question. In
gratitude I ask you to help my teachers so that
they can continue to help me. Be close to me and
teach me to enjoy learning and to do my best.
Amen.

Prayerbook: A Catholic Religious Site

A Child's Prayer of Thanksgiving

Dear God, I thank you for all good things; for my
home, for food and clothes, for my friends, for
my toys and books and fun and everything. Help
me to share all my good things with others.
Amen.

Prayerbook: A Catholic Religious Site

Prayer to the Trinity

Praise to the Father.
Praise to the Son.
Praise to the Spirit.
The Three in One.

Paidir don Tríonóid Naofa

Moladh don Athair,
Agus don Mhac,
Agus don Spiorad Naomh,
An triúr ina aon.

Alive-O/Beo go Deo

'Let's Pray' Prayers from *Alive-O*
God, you know me.
You love me.
You call me by my name.
Amen.

Thank you, God, for me.
Thank you, God, for others.
Friends, relations, sisters,
Brothers, fathers, mothers.

At school or at home God is there.
God is with us everywhere.
Amen.

Thank you, God, for the people
who work so school can be
a place that's clean and bright and warm
and fun for you and me.

Thank you, God, for me.
I am special.

God bless mothers.
God bless fathers.
God bless babies.
God bless everyone.
Amen.

We remember that God is with us at all times.
God is with us every time we laugh,
every time we cry, every time we talk,
every time we sing, every time we play.
God is with us at all times all through the day.
We give God thanks.

From the time it came to be
I have been there.

Is 48:16

'Pray Together' Prayers from *Alive-O*
Thank you, God, for the church where we come
together with our friends and family to pray.

Time and time and time again,
praise God, praise God.

God you are our light in times of sadness and in
times of happiness.

Thank you, God, for all the goodness inside me.
Help me always to be good in all I do and say.

We praise you. We bless you.
We thank you.

For the air we share as we breathe together,
for the food we share as we eat together,
for the love we share as we live together,
we praise you, O God, and we bless you.

May all I say and do,
May all I do and say
Show your love, Lord Jesus,
Every moment of every day.

God our Creator, we ask you to look
with favour on the work we offer you.
May your Holy Spirit help us and guide us
in working together.

SECTION THREE

FAMILY PRAYERS
FOR ALL OCCASIONS

Prayers for an Engaged Couple

May our love increasingly be a sign of Christ's love for the Church.
Let our daily nurturing of our relationship use the Mass as a model.

Let us each day humbly acknowledge our faults and ask for forgiveness for any hurts we have caused the other.
May we take any opportunity for praising and affirming the talents and efforts of the other.
May we offer our time, understanding and active, empathetic listening even when we judge that we have heard before what we are hearing now.
May we pray with and for each other in whatever ways we can.

May we try to build a solid foundation of openness and trust based upon similar values.

May we celebrate our coming vows and put the stress on our relationship building not on the wedding day details that will soon pale in importance.

May we treat each other with a sacred trust that
seeks to build up.
Help us believe that God sends us forth as a
couple
To become an ever clearer channel of his love.
Don't let us neglect to give each other a kiss of
peace often!
May we go in peace to love and serve the Lord.

Kathy and Kevin Misiewicz

Lord our God,
pour out your blessings on N. and N. In your
providence you have brought them together.
Help them to prepare well for their marriage.
Bring them closer to each other in respect and
trust.
As you have given them to each other,
help them to give themselves to you.
May your love be upon them as they place all
their hope in you.
We ask this through Christ, our Lord.
Amen.

The Veritas Book of Blessing Prayers

Prayer of the Newly Married Couple
We thank you, Lord,
and we praise you
for bringing us
to this happy day.

You have given us to each other.
Now, together, we give ourselves to you.

We ask you, Lord:
make us one in your love;
keep us one in your peace.

Protect our marriage.
Bless our home.
Make us gentle.
Keep us faithful.

And when life is over
unite us again
where parting is no more
in the kingdom of your love.

There we will praise you
in the happiness and peace
of our eternal home.
Amen.

The Celebration of Marriage Within Mass

❖ ❖ ❖

For Newlyweds

Blessed are you,
O Lord our God, king of the universe;
we bless you each day of our married life.
Renew your blessing within us
as we choose each day, by your grace,
to be a living sign of your eternal love;
may we come to know, love, accept,
forgive, and encourage each other anew.
We ask you to guide us today, as ...
(either or both could mention whatever situation
seems important)
for the kingdom, the power, and the glory are
yours now and for ever. Amen.

The Veritas Book of Blessing Prayers

Prayers for Married Couples

Help us Lord to be witnesses for marriage to the couples we meet and our children. Strengthen us to deal with the day-to-day living of the Sacrament of Marriage and to be a support to all those on the spiritual journey whether they are assured or struggling.

Stephen Cummins

God of love, we praise and thank you
For the privilege of
Knowing you and loving you.
Thank you for this time
Spent in your presence.
Bless all those we have thought about
And prayed for during this time.
Bless all married couples.
Help them to rejoice in their love today.
Be with all families so that your love
And peace may be in all our homes.
And bless all of us so that
Your will may become ours,
Your name may be held holy,
And your kingdom may
Be established in our world.
We ask this through Christ our Lord.
Amen.

Johnny Doherty CSsR

In Support of Couples

All powerful and ever living God,
Your will is that no one should have
to go through life without knowing how special
they are,
how treasured and loved they are.

We ask you to forgive us for failing so many
people
in their journey through life.
Bless all those who give themselves so generously
in helping husbands and wives to renew
their love constantly so that
through each other they may know your love.

We ask your blessing on those
who work at helping parents and their children to
develop
a good communication so that understanding and
love may grow
in our homes and each person be reverenced as he
or she is.

And we pray for an outpouring
of your Spirit on those who are engaged in
bringing healing to the people who are
damaged because of their experiences
in marriage or family life.

Inspire all leaders of church and state to know
more clearly
that it is in marriage and family life especially that
human life has its greatest potential
and that it is in these relationships that we can
come to know your
presence and love in a special way.
We make our prayer through Christ our Lord.
Amen.

Johnny Doherty CSsR

For All Married Couples

God of love, in your wonderful love for us you
have made
the love of woman and man the mirror of your
everlasting love.
May we reverence all married couples and make it
possible for them to
grow in their love every day.
Bless all young married couples.
May their passion for each other grow through
their lives,
be with couples who are a few years into
marriage.
Give them a great commitment to each other as
they learn to cope with
and master the ever-changing decisions they need
to make together.
Keep them faithful to each other and to you.
Journey with all married couples who are entering
mid life together.
Give them a real affection for one another.
Keep them open to one another and to all around
them.
May their love become an ever greater gift to the
Church.
And we pray for couples who are entering into
old age together.
Keep them young at heart, confident in their love
for each other
and your presence with them.

Keep all couples aware of the importance to love
fully in the present
so that our world may be transformed
by the radiance of married love.
we ask this through Christ our Lord.
Amen.

Johnny Doherty CSsR

For Couples

We thank you, O God, for the love you have
implanted in our hearts.
May it inspire us to be kind in our words,
considerate of feelings and concerned with each
other's feelings and wishes.
Help us to be understanding and forgiving of
human weakness and failings.
Bless our marriage, O God, with peace and
happiness, and make our love fruitful for your
glory and our joy both here and in eternity.

Stephen Cummins

Litany of Blessing (adapted from an old Irish blessing)

> May God bless this house.
> May the Holy Spirit bless this house.
> May the Holy Trinity bless this house.
> May Mary bless this house.
> May Archangel Michael bless this house.
> May the holy apostles and martyrs bless this house.
> Both mortar and construction.
> Both stone and timber.
> Both crest and frame.
> Both top and foundation.
> Both window and woodwork.
> Both floor and roof.
> Both husband and wife.
> (Both parents and children.)
> Both young and old.
> May the King of the elements preserve it.
> May the King of glory take charge of it.
> May Christ, the gentle son of Mary,
> pour out the graces of his Holy Spirit on it.
> Amen.

The Veritas Book of Blessing Prayers

 ❖ ❖ ❖

Bless This House

Bless this house O Lord we pray,
Make it safe by night and day,
Bless these walls so firm and stout,
keeping want and trouble out.
Bless this roof and chimneys tall,
let thy peace lie over all.
Bless this door that it may prove
Ever open to joy and love.
Bless the windows shining bright
letting in God's heavenly light.
Bless the hearth ablazing there with
smoke ascending like a prayer.
Bless the people here within
Keep them pure and free from sin.
Bless us Lord that we may be fit
O Lord to dwell with thee.
Bless us all that we may one day
dwell O Lord with thee.

Helen Taylor & May H. Brahe

Hospitality

Help us Jesus in our family life
to share your hospitality always,
opening our homes and still more
of each of our hearts to the pleas
of our brothers and sisters,
in concrete efforts,
welcoming the brother or sister
in need.

Rev Peter Murphy,
inspired by John Paul II, *Familiaris Consortio*, n.44

For a Married Couple Before Becoming Parents

Lord, often our worries about the responsibilities
of being parents make us forget that on the day of
our marriage you united us as a married couple,
in a unique relationship full of fidelity, sincerity
and communion.

We don't always find time for ourselves,
and so at times we struggle to understand and
dialogue.
Sometimes we seem to argue easily,
or we get on with the routine of doing things
without reflecting on what we are doing.
We become impoverished inside and begin to feel
empty.

Lord help us to re-discover that before we are
mother and father we are husband and wife.
Help us to grow in mutual and joyful love.

In our total openness to love and to life itself
we know that without giving our living love to
one another we cannot give love to our loved ones
and those around us.

Give us that newness once again which came with
our initial hopes,
while drawing on the wisdom of maturity that
comes with time.
Help us to value and appreciate the great gift of
being a married couple
blessed by you in our Sacrament of Marriage.

Rev Peter Murphy

❖ ❖ ❖

Choose Life: Prayer for the Child in the Womb

Lord Jesus, you are the source and lover of life.
Reawaken in us respect for every human life.

Help us to see in each child the marvellous work
of our Creator.
Open our hearts to welcome every child as a
unique and wonderful gift.

Guide the work of doctors, nurses and midwives.
May the life of a mother and her baby in the
womb be equally cherished and respected.

Help those who make our laws to uphold the
uniqueness and sacredness of every human life,
from the first moment of conception to natural
death.

Give us wisdom and generosity to build a society
that cares for all.

Together with Mary, your Mother,
in whose womb you took on our human nature,
Help us to choose life in every decision we take.

We ask this in the joyful hope of eternal life with
you, and in the communion of the
Blessed Trinity. Amen.

Our Lady of Knock, *pray for us*.
All the saints of Ireland, *pray for us*.

Irish Catholic Bishops' Conference, 2012

Prayer from *Evangelium Vitae*

O Mary,
bright dawn of the new world,
Mother of the living,
to you do we entrust the cause of life.
Look down, O Mother,
upon the vast numbers
of babies not allowed to be born,
of the poor whose lives are made difficult,
of men and women
who are victims of brutal violence,
of the elderly and the sick killed
by indifference or out of misguided mercy.

Grant that all who believe in your Son
may proclaim the gospel of life
with honesty and love
to the people of our time.

Obtain for them the grace
to accept that gospel
as a gift ever new,
the joy of celebrating it with gratitude
throughout their lives
and the courage to bear witness to it
resolutely, in order to build,
together with all people of good will,
the civilization of truth and love,
to the praise and glory of God,
the Creator and lover of life.

John Paul II, *Evangelium Vitae*, 25 March 1995

❖ ❖ ❖

For a Newborn

Watch over this child, O Lord as their days
increase,
Be a source of blessing and guidance in all that
they do.
Pick them up if they should fall,
comfort them when they are discouraged or
sorrowful
grant them peace in their heart all the days of
their life.
Through Jesus Christ, our Lord. Amen.

Stephen Cummins

For Our Children

We pray for our children, wherever they may be,
asking Jesus, Mary and Joseph to watch over and
guard them throughout their lives and that the
faith we have passed on to them may sustain
them through all that life will put before them.

Stephen Cummins

Children's First Experience of the Family of the Church

As parents,
through the witness of our lives,
we are the first heralds of the gospel
for our children.

Guide us and be with us Jesus
as we pray with our children,
read the word of God with them
and as we introduce them
into the body of Christ, the family of the Church.

Rev Peter Murphy,
inspired by John Paul II, *Familiaris Consortio*, n.39

Children, the Precious Gift of Marriage

Loving and mysterious God,
in our marriage as we give ourselves
to one another as a couple
and to the possibility of becoming
in love co-operators with you for giving life
to a new human person,
help us if we receive the gift of this new
responsibility,
to be always a visible sign of your very love.

Rev Peter Murphy,
inspired by John Paul II, *Familiaris Consortio*, n.14

The Broader Communion of the Family

Lord,
guide us and help us as a communion
of persons in our family to deepen our humanity
in the care for the little ones,
the sick, the aged,
in our mutual service every day
and in our sharing
of goods, of joys and of sorrows.

Rev Peter Murphy,
inspired by John Paul II, Familiaris Consortio, n.21

For Children (by Parents)

Blessed are you, Lord God,
giver of life and love;
we thank you for the gift of our children;
may they grow before you in wisdom and grace;
through Christ our Lord.
Amen.

The Veritas Book of Blessing Prayers

Mother's Day

Thank you Lord for all mothers. On this day let us think of them,

whether they are with us or gone to their heavenly reward.

We think of their kindness, their compassion, their care for us and above all their unconditional love.

We pray that you will watch over them and support them in the joys and struggles of their daily lives.

This we ask through Christ, our Lord. Amen.

Stephen Cummins

Father's Day

Heavenly Father, you have been pleased to let me be called the name that is yours for all eternity. Help me to be worthy of that name.

Let me offer good example to my children in all situations of life.

Grant me wisdom and strength and love and let me be conscious that

my actions speak louder than my words.

May I support them in their growth as human persons, fulfilling my duty to guide them in the ways given to us by your Son Jesus Christ. Amen.

Stephen Cummins

Fathers and Mothers

Dear Lord, we who are fathers and mothers need
your help.
You have placed in us the care of each other and
of our children.
Give us the strength and patience to cope with
the many ups and downs of family life.
Grant us the grace to be deeply thankful for its
many laughs, joys and blessings.
Let our children come to know of your love
through our love for them.
Help us as we try to make ours a home where love
dwells, a home like that of Jesus, Mary and Joseph
in Nazareth.
When we fail each other and when we hurt each
other, soften our hearts so that forgiveness and
reconciliation comes quickly and easily.

Protect this family, Lord, and let it flourish in
your light and in your love. We ask this through
Christ our Lord. Amen.

The Veritas Book of Blessing Prayers

A Husband's Prayer

Dear Lord, help me to be the best possible
husband for my wife.
Let me be a source of strength and love, a
listening ear, offering a caring touch, and above
all else a partner sharing all that life will offer.
Amen.

Stephen Cummins

A Wife's Prayer

I pray Lord, that I will be the best possible wife
for my husband. Help me to be a source of
strength, a listening ear, offering a caring touch,
and above all a partner in all that my husband
and I will face together in our married life, with
your help and guidance. Through Christ our
Lord. Amen.

Stephen Cummins

Universal Prayer for Grandparents

Lord Jesus,
you were born of the Virgin Mary,
the daughter of Saints Joachim and Anne.
Look with love on grandparents the world over.
Protect them! They are a source of enrichment
for families, for the Church and for all of society.
Support them! As they grow older,
may they continue to be for their families
strong pillars of Gospel faith,
guardian of noble domestic ideals,
living treasuries of sound religious traditions.
Make them teachers of wisdom and courage,
that they may pass on to future generations the fruits
of their mature human and spiritual experience.

Lord Jesus,
help families and society
to value the presence and roles of grandparents.
May they never be ignored or excluded,
but always encounter respect and love.
Help them to live serenely and to feel welcomed
in all the years of life which you give them.
Mary, Mother of all the living,
keep grandparents constantly in your care,
accompany them on their earthly pilgrimage,
and by your prayers, grant that all families
may one day be reunited in our heavenly homeland,
where you await all humanity
for the great embrace of life without end. Amen!

Pope Benedict XVI, The Catholic Grandparents Association 2008

An Elderly Person

Eternal God,
we thank you for the long life of N.
May your continual blessing be upon her/him
and your peace in her/his heart.
Grant her/him cheerfulness in good health
and patience in times of bad.
When she/he worries about the past
give her/him trust in your abiding mercy:
and when she/he fears for the future
grant her/him trust and hope.
Let courage and wisdom guide her/him daily.
May her/his family, friends and neighbours
be blessed in their support of her/him.
May the risen Lord Jesus be her/his companion
on the way;
and stay with her/him when it is towards evening
and the day is far spent.
May almighty God bless you,
the Father, and the Son, ✠ and the Holy Spirit.
Amen.

The Veritas Book of Blessing Prayers

A Prayer for Irish Emigrants

Lord, some may know the bleakness of life,
its capacity to disappoint,
the waning of energy or health.
Yet they have a place in the soul which time
cannot touch,
a wisdom and beauty from lives deeply inhabited.
May all of them know the warmth of their soul,
the natural shelter around their lives.
In dignity and freedom,
may they return home to themselves.
Amen.

Anon

A Prayer for Immigrants

Blessed are you, Lord Jesus Christ.
You crossed every border between divinity and
humanity to make your home with us.
Help us to welcome you in newcomers, migrants
and refugees.

Blessed are you, God of all nations.
You bless our land richly with goods of creation
and with people made in your image.
Help us to be good stewards and peacemakers,
who live as your children.

Blessed are you, Holy Spirit.
You work in the hearts of all to bring about
harmony and goodwill.
Strengthen us to welcome those from other lands,
cultures, religions,
that we may live in human solidarity and in hope.

God of all people,
grant us vision to see your presence in our midst,
especially in our immigrant sisters and brothers.
Give us courage to open the door to our
neighbours
and grace to build a society of justice.

Pax Christi

A Birthday Blessing

We bless you, heavenly Father,
as we celebrate the birthday of N.
We thank you for the gift of life,
for the blessings of these … years,
and for giving us this day of joy.
N., may God fill your heart with his peace,
keep you in his loving care,
and bring you safely through the years to come.
We ask this through Christ out Lord.
Amen.

The Veritas Book of Blessing Prayers

Birthday Prayers

On this your birthday, I pray for you in a special
way.
I thank God for your uniqueness and the many
gifts he has given you.
I pray that with each passing year you grow closer
to God getting to know him
as friend and wishing you long life and happiness.

Stephen Cummins

On this your special day, I pray for you.
I pray for your happiness, for friends that are
faithful.
I pray for warmth and tenderness.
I pray for many moments of joy and laughter,
for continuous good health.
But most of all, I pray that God will visit you this
day
and remain with you forever.

Stephen Cummins

Wedding Anniversary

Living God,
you created man and woman
to love each other
in the bond of marriage
Bless and strengthen N. and N.
May their marriage become an increasingly more
perfect sign of the union between Christ and his
Church.
We ask this through Christ our Lord. Amen.

The Veritas Book of Blessing Prayers

Silver Wedding Anniversary

Father,
you have blessed and sustained N. and N.
in the bond of marriage.
Continue to increase their love
throughout the joys of their married life
and help them to grow in holiness all their days.
We ask this through Christ our Lord. Amen.

The Veritas Book of Blessing Prayers

Golden Wedding Anniversary

God, our Father
bless N. and N.
We thank you for their long and happy marriage
(for the children they have brought into the world)
and for all the good they have done.
As you blessed the love of their youth
continue to bless their life together
with gifts of peace and joy.
We ask this through Christ our Lord. Amen.

The Veritas Book of Blessing Prayers

Wedding Anniversary

Lord, we thank you for our wedding anniversary.

Many situations shared:
Joys, troubles, surprises, hopes,
mistakes and beginning again.

How many of our relations and friends are
connected to our story as a married couple and as
a family.
We are indebted to them.
To all we wish your blessings.

Forgive us for any of our failings or our
omissions.
Make fruitful our choices to walk together.

You, as source of true love and fidelity,
inspire our gestures
guide our moments of communion.
So that we are always a sign of your presence.

Rev Peter Murphy

Prayer to St Valentine

O glorious advocate and protector,
St Valentine,
look with pity upon our wants,
hear our requests,
attend to our prayers,
relieve by your intercession the miseries
under which we labour,
and obtain for us the divine blessing,
that we may be found worthy to join you
in praising the Almighty for all eternity:
through the merits of
Our Lord Jesus Christ.
Amen.

Whitefriar Street Parish, Dublin

A Valentine Prayer

I said a Valentine prayer for you
And asked the Lord above
To fill your heart and bless your soul
With the precious gift of love.

I asked him for sincere love
The kind that's meant to stay
Just like the generous love
You give to those you touch each day.

I prayed for love from family
And from every cherished friend
Then I asked the Lord to give you
His love that knows no end.

Catholic Online

Changes On Our Journey

My love, let us love each other always
even when things change
because of health or sickness.
Let us remain in love and in dignity.

If I am old or weak or weary or difficult,
do not become nervous or give up on me.

I pray with you in the Lord
that you will find
– strength for your burden
– a way to listen and to be patient and
that you will receive support as you
support me.

Work at continuing to love and understand me as
we have always struggled to do together, loving
one another. Amen.

Rev Peter Murphy, *World Day of the Sick Prayerbook,* 2013

Blessing Upon Retirement

    Blessed are you, Lord God of all creation,
    for through your goodness you have given us
    the gift of labour and fruitful productivity
    that your people may thrive and grow.
    You invite us to be co-workers with you in the
    world,
    to join the fruit of the earth with the work of our
    hands
    that we may create something new for the good of
    others.
    We thank you and bless you for the dignity of
    work,
    which has called forth from us unknown skills
    and talents.

    Yet you call us also to come to you,
    we who labour and are heavy-burdened,
    for work without rest is enslavement
    and a forgetfulness of our dependence upon you
    alone.

    So look with favour now upon your faithful
    servant, N.,
    who has laboured long days in your vineyard
    and now enters a new way of using the time and
    talents you have given him/her.

Bless him/her with eyes to see the places where
he/she is most needed,
with ears to listen to others with the luxury of
time,
with hands that create for the simple joy of
creating,
and with hearts lifted from the burden of toil.

Remove any fear of feeling useless or unwanted,
protect him/her from boredom and despair,
and free him/her from all anxiety.

May he/she know that his/her worth and dignity
are not measured by what he/she does
but by who he/she is in your eyes,
your precious child and our beloved
brother/sister.

And when each day is ended,
may he/she find delight in knowing that
God who has begun the good work in him/her
will bring it to completion in Christ Jesus, our
Lord. Amen.

Catholic Online

God's Plan for Our Marriage and Family

As we answer God's call
in our vocation
in the Sacrament of Marriage
to follow Christ and to serve
the kingdom of God in our married life,
we ask, in and through the concreteness of
events, problems, difficulties and circumstances
of everyday life, that God will come to us,
guiding us and enlightening us as we share
Christ's love with one another, in our family life,
at work, in our neighbourhood, in our
contributions to society
and in the life and worship of our parish.

Rev Peter Murphy,
inspired by John Paul II, *Familiaris Consortio*, n.51

Living in Justice and in Love

O Lord,
the Christian family
is the first community
called to live together the gospel.

Let us always help one another to discern
our own vocations and to accept responsibility
in the search for greater justice
and in our interpersonal relationships
to be rich in justice and in love.

Rev Peter Murphy,
inspired by John Paul II, *Familiaris Consortio*, n.2

General Blessing for a Family or Household

O God,
You have created us in love and saved us in mercy,
and through the bond of marriage
you have established the family
and willed that it should become a sign
of Christ's love for his Church.

Shower your blessings on this family
gathered here in your name.
Enable those who are joined by one love
to support one another
by their fervor of spirit and devotion to prayer.
Make them responsive to the needs of others
and witnesses to the faith in all they say and do.
We ask this through Christ our Lord.
Amen.

Catholic Household Blessings and Prayers, p. 186

Blessing for a Family and their Home

The grace and peace of God our Father and of
our Lord Jesus Christ be with you all.
And with your Spirit.

We welcome the visit of Jesus the Good Shepherd
who enters into our house and home and gives us
his gift of joy and his peace.

The Word of God is a particular sign of his
presence among us.
The grace of the Holy Spirit allows our hearts to
be open to Jesus, who comes to speak to us and to
bring to life our Faith.
Amen.

Reawaken in us Lord, in the sign of the cross with
this holy water, the memory of our Baptism and
our membership into Jesus Christ and his family
the Church.
Amen.

God our Father, fill us with every joy and hope in
the faith.
May the Peace of Jesus live always in our hearts.
May the Holy Spirit give us an abundance of your
gifts.
Amen.

Rev Peter Murphy

For Families

    Holy Trinity, Father, Son and Spirit,
    We praise you and worship you.
    You are the origin of all life.
    You are the source of all love.
    We thank you for sharing your life
    and your love with us, your people.
    We pray for all families made in your image.
    Unite all couples and fill them
    with enthusiasm for their love.
    Bless all families so that parents may treasure
    the children of all ages
    and that children may grow in affection
    and love for their parents and for one another.
    Be with those who are alone.
    Help them to know their beauty and goodness
    and give them peace in their times
    of loneliness or isolation.
    Fill every home with your love.
    May each of our homes be places
    of your presence and sources of your peace.
    Amen.

Johnny Doherty CSsR

Family Times and Moments of Friendship

As we remember good times when
our loved ones helped us on our way
– times of togetherness, family times
and moments of friendship –

Let us continue to cherish each one
and to do for one another
whatever we can, with generosity,
recalling what was done for us.

O Lord, help us to continue
to love one another. Amen.

Rev Peter Murphy, *World Day of the Sick Prayerbook*, 2013

The Family

Blessed are you, Lord our God, giver of life:
give your strength and wisdom to the father of
this family.
Blessed are you, Holy Spirit, bearer of love:
give your compassion and understanding to the
mother of this family.
Blessed are you, Son of God, eternal wisdom:
give your knowledge and truth to the children of
this family.
(Blessed are you, Holy Trinity, eternal and
almighty: shadow with your protecting wings the
absent/departed members of this family.)

Father, we want to live as Jesus, Mary and Joseph,
in peace with you and with one another.
By following their example in mutual love and
respect may we come to the joy of our home in
heaven.
We ask this through Christ our Lord.
Amen.

May the Lord bless you and keep you.
May his face shine upon you and be gracious to
you.
May he look upon you with kindness, and give
his peace.
May almighty God bless you, the Father and Son,
✠ and the Holy Spirit. Amen.

The Veritas Book of Blessing Prayers

❖ ❖ ❖

Prayers for Families

Lord, we thank you for our family.
Bless each one of us in our uniqueness
and let us use our gifts and talents to ensure
unity and love within our family now and always.
Amen.

Stephen Cummins

Lord, you chose to enter the world as a member
of a family. Take care of all families. May they be
sources of love and security for all family
members, where each person is valued and given
the chance to reach their full potential.

Stephen Cummins

For all our families, who welcome Christ into
their lives; that they learn to receive him in the
poor and suffering people of this world.

Stephen Cummins

A Family Prayer

> God our Father,
> your Son, Jesus Christ,
> is our Way, our Truth and our Life.
>
> His way of being human shapes our
> understanding of the human person and
> of human relationships of every kind.
>
> In a special way it shapes our
> understanding of ourselves as a family.
>
> Trying to live as Jesus lived –
> respectful, forgiving, helpful and
> caring towards one another –
> is a daily challenge to every person
> in this family of ours.
>
> We are in constant need of your
> forgiveness and help. May your
> Holy Spirit – the Spirit of Jesus
> himself – bind us together in love.
>
> Together, as a family, may we face with
> hope and confidence whatever suffering or
> sorrow may come our way.

May our hearts be ever open to the needs
of other families and individuals
everywhere in our world.

We make this prayer through
Christ our Lord.
Amen.

Diocese of Elphin

SECTION FOUR

IN TIMES OF NEED
AND DIFFICULTY

Jesus, You Are With Me

Jesus, you give us the hope of eternal life.
I trust in you as you guide me safely through life.
In my experience of emptiness, insecurity,
and fear, I turn to you in your everlasting love
and friendship for me and for every person.
As I ask myself where am I to go and what
can I do, I come to you because you have
promised to be with me always.
Jesus, I trust in your never failing mercy and love.
I know how much you love me.
You healed the sick, the deaf, the lame and the
blind.
As I turn to you, I ask for healing and strength.
In my faith in you, I hear your words, 'Don't be
afraid' (Luke 8:50).
Jesus, strengthen my faith.

Rev Peter Murphy, *World Day of the Sick Prayerbook,* 2013

For Parents of a Sick Child

Lord, bless the parents of N.
who come to you in their need.
They are thankful for all the time
when their child was strong and healthy.
They take comfort from the love
you have always shown to children:
remembering how you restored to life
the son of the widow of Nain
and the daughter of Jairus.

Give them courage to hide their worry and anxiety
as they try to soothe their child's pain.
Let them see that in this illness
they can come closer to you and to one another.
We join with them in praying with all our hearts
that you may heal their child.
Grant each of us the grace to say at all times,
'Welcome to your holy will'.
We make our prayer through Christ our Lord.
Amen.

The Veritas Book of Blessing Prayers

For One Ill in Hospital
All-powerful and ever-living God,
the lasting health of all who believe in you
hear us as we ask your loving help for the sick;
restore their health,
that they may again offer joyful thanks in your
Church.
We ask this through Christ, our Lord.
Amen.

The Veritas Book of Blessing Prayers

Parents Who Have Suffered a Miscarriage

    Lord God,
    ever caring and gentle,
    we commit to your love this little one,
    quickened to life for so short a time.

    Bless these parents
    who are saddened by the loss of their baby.
    Give them courage
    and help them in their pain and grief.
    May they all meet one day
    in the joy and peace of your kingdom.
    We ask this through Christ our Lord. Amen.

The Veritas Book of Blessing Prayers

For Carers

> For each person in my care,
> O loving and mysterious God,
> Open my heart to their healing need.
> Strengthen me.
> Give me wisdom as you guide me
> in my care for the sick.
> Help me to see the presence
> of the suffering and risen Jesus
> in each person and to know always
> that you look at me, O Lord,
> through the eyes of the sick
> and that you love each of us as we give and receive
> care from each other. Amen.

World Day of the Sick Prayerbook, 2013

A Prayer for a Family Affected by Addiction

Father in Heaven,
I come before you today as a member of a family.
As I take this moment to think of each
member of my family, I thank you for the
blessings they bring to me. I know that
every family is different and sometimes I can
get frustrated at the family you have given to me.
May I learn to appreciate them through the bad
times as well as the good and, as I grow, may
my relationship with my family also grow in
strength and love.
Amen.

Prayerbook for Those Affected by Addiction

Prayer for Students Taking Exams

Lord, pour out your Spirit of Wisdom on these
students:
help them to remain calm,
to attend carefully to the questions asked,
to think clearly, to remember accurately,
and to express themselves well.

Grant that they may reflect the best of the work
they have done
and the best of the teaching they have received.
Accept their best efforts in these examinations
and in the great test of life on earth.
May your love be upon them, O Lord,
as they place all their trust in you.

We ask this through Christ our Lord.
Amen.

The Veritas Book of Blessing Prayers

Missing Persons

God our Father,
your Son Jesus Christ as a child
was lost in the chaos of a great city
and was restored to the love of his family;
watch over N., now missing, for whom we pray
and protect him/her with your love.
Be near to those who are anxious for him/her;
let your presence change their sorrow into
comfort,
their anxiety into trust,
their despair into faith,
that they may know your loving purposes.
And this we ask
in the name of Jesus our Lord,
who loves and lives
and cares for all your children. Amen.

Blessing
May Christ draw you to himself
that you may find in his cross
a sure ground for faith
and a firm support for hope:
and the blessing of God almighty,
the Father, the Son, and the Holy Spirit,
be with you and remain with you always. Amen.

The Veritas Book of Blessing Prayers

❖ ❖ ❖

Lend Me Your Hand

Jesus, remember me
at this time.
I have questions and concerns.
I am worried.
As you journey with me, Jesus,
in your promise
of everlasting friendship,
help me to place myself
in your care
as you lend me your hand
through the care of my carers.
Help us, Jesus, to allow God's Light
to shine through our hopes and concerns.

Rev Peter Murphy, *World Day of the Sick Prayerbook,* 2013

Prayer to Our Lady

Mother Mary, at the wedding feast of Cana you
interceded with Jesus for the couple in their need.
Please intercede now with your divine son for my
needs and the needs of all the members of my
family.

Stephen Cummins

A Prayer at Night (Psalm 4)

> When I call,
> answer me, O God of justice;
> from anguish you released me,
> have mercy and hear me!
> … Make justice your sacrifice and trust in the
> Lord.
> 'What can bring us happiness?' many say.
> Lift up the light of your face, O Lord.
> You have put into my heart a greater joy …
> For you alone, Lord, make me dwell in safety.

Grail Psalms

Be Like the Good Samaritan

May the Holy Virgin comfort
those who are afflicted by illness
and support those who,
like the Good Samaritan,
soothe their physical and spiritual wounds.
I assure each of you
that you will be remembered in my prayer.

Prayer for those who are sick and for all who care for the sick by
Pope Benedict XVI, 14th World Day of the Sick, 11 February 2005

Prayer in Time of Pain or Difficulty

Lord Jesus,
Help us to carry the weight of the Cross,
as you carried it
abandoned into the hands of your Father.

Help us to remain connected with you,
help us to live suffering
as you have lived it,
with faith, hope and love.

Give us the inner strength
to overcome the pain
with a peaceful trust of abandonment
knowing that suffering is not wasted
if it is united to the cross
sign of your total love
for all people.

Rev Peter Murphy

Prayer with the Dying

Go forth, Christian soul, from this world
In the name of God the almighty Father,
Who created you,
In the name of Jesus Christ, Son of the living
God, who suffered for you,
In the name of the Holy Spirit,
Who was poured out upon you,
Go forth, faithful Christian.

May you live in peace this day,
May your home be with God in Zion,
With Mary, the Virgin Mother of God,
With Joseph, and all the angels and saints

Catholic Household Blessings and Prayers, p. 267

For a Widow or Widower

Those whom we love and lose are no longer
where they were before. They are now wherever
we are.

St John Chrysostom

Eternal God and Father,
whose love is stronger than death,
look with pity on our sister/brother whose
marriage was a figure
of the union of Christ with his Church.
She/he is desolate now without the companion
you gave her/him in that holy sacrament.
Comfort her/him with your presence
and the indwelling of your Holy Spirit.
Keep her/him in the joyful hope
of one day being reunited with her/his loved one
in your heavenly dwelling place.

We ask this through Christ our Lord.

Blessing
May the blessing of almighty God,
the Father, the Son, ✠ and the Holy Spirit,
rest upon you;
may he give light to guide you,
courage to support you,
and love to unite you,
now and for evermore. Amen.

The Veritas Book of Blessing Prayers

The Recently Bereaved

God, loving Father,
be close to those who are mourning the loss of
one so dear to them.
Heal the pain they now suffer,
lighten their darkness,
and scatter the doubts that their grief brings.
Let the remembrance
of how your Son Jesus wept at the death of
Lazarus his friend be a consolation to them at this
time.

May they feel Christ's healing power come to
them in their pain and distress.

Give them the strength to keep on going forward
with faith as their consolation
and eternal life as their hope.

Grant everlasting rest and peace to the one they
loved.
May they keep the memory of their joy in
him/her ever fresh.
Grant that we may all be gathered together again
in the joy of your Kingdom with the Virgin Mary
and all the saints.
We ask this through Christ our Lord. Amen.

May almighty God bless you,
the Father, and the Son, ✠ and the Holy Spirit.
Amen.

The Veritas Book of Blessing Prayers

❖ ❖ ❖

Prayer for the Dead

Into your hands, O Lord,
We humbly entrust our brothers and sisters.
In this life you embraced them with your tender
love;
deliver them now from every evil
and bid them enter eternal rest.

The old order has passed away:
welcome them into paradise,
where there will be no sorrow,
no weeping nor pain,
but fullness of peace and joy
with your Son and the Holy Spirit
forever and ever.
Amen.

Catholic Household Blessings and Prayers, p. 268

We Give Them Back to Thee, O God

We seem to give them back to thee,
O God, who givest them to us.
Yet, as thou didst not lose them
in the giving, so do we not lose them
by their return.
Not as the world giveth thou,
O Lover of souls.
What thou givest, thou takest not away.
For what is thine is ours also, if we are thine.
Life is eternal. Love is immortal.
Death is only an horizon and
horizon is only the limit of the sight.
Lift us up, O Strong Son of God,
that we may see further.
Cleanse our eyes that we may
see more clearly.
Draw us closer to thyself,
that we may know ourselves to be nearer
to our loved ones who are with thee.
And while thou dost prepare a place for us,
prepare us for that happy place
that where thou art, we may be also forever.
Amen.

Bede Jarrett OP

For a Father Who Has Died

I thank you God for my father. He was my
inspiration, my strength, my teacher and I loved
him dearly. You were at the heart of all that he did
and his daily life bore witness to his faith. Grant
him peace and happiness in your kingdom as a
reward for all his work. I pray that I may be worthy
to be re-united with him one day in heaven.

Stephen Cummins

For a Mother Who Has Died

I commit my mother to your care, O Lord. She
was my inspiration, my carer, a dear friend and a
constant source of love and affection. Grant unto
her, O Lord, eternal rest and happiness as a
reward for all she did not just for me but for all
with whom she came into contact.

Stephen Cummins

In Remembrance

No person is ever truly alone.
Those who live no more, whom we loved,
echo still within our thoughts, our words, our
hearts.
And what they did and who they were
becomes part of what we are forever.

Stephen Cummins

On the Loss of a Husband or Wife

God of love and compassion, we ask your
special blessing on those among us
who have lost a wife or husband in any way.
They all set out with high ambitions.
Many now live in disappointment or deep
loneliness
or anger or despair.
Reach into their hearts and lives
and bring them to healing.
We ask you to comfort those who are alone
through death.
We ask you to strengthen those whose spouse
is seriously ill;
to inspire those whose communication has
broken down and give them courage to begin again.
And we pray for those whose marriages
have broken down.
Help them to find the ways back to
health of body and spirit.
Give those around them a generous love
and a caring understanding so that
they will be supported as they need,
And prompt those who may be moving in
the direction of break up to see what is happening
and to do everything that is needed to prevent it.
We ask this through Christ our Lord. Amen.

Johnny Doherty CSsR

❖ ❖ ❖

SECTION FIVE

SEASONS, VALUES AND REFLECTIONS

Advent

Lord Jesus, Master of both the light and the darkness, send your Holy Spirit upon our preparations for Christmas.
We who have so much to do seek quiet spaces to hear your voice each day.
We who are anxious over many things look forward to your coming among us.
We who are blessed in so many ways long for the complete joy of your kingdom.
We whose hearts are heavy seek the joy of your presence.
We are your people, walking in darkness, yet seeking the light. To you we say, 'Come Lord Jesus!'

Henri Nouwen

Advent Wreath

Today we begin preparing to celebrate, with hope-filled joy, the coming of the Lord at Christmas. We ask God's blessing on this wreath of evergreens.

The Word was the real light
that gives light to everyone;
he was coming into the world
from his fullness, we have, all of us, received.

Jn 1:9-16

Father, all powerful Lord of Light, bless our wreath of evergreens with its candles.

May our Advent be a time of preparation. Help us reflect on the power of light to dispel darkness in our world and in our lives. Touch our hearts with the warmth of your love. May the increasing light of these candles brighten our minds and hearts to be steadfast in faith, joyful in hope and untiring in love, so that we are ready again to receive in true peace, Jesus, the Light of the World, our Lord and Saviour. Amen.

The Veritas Book of Blessing Prayers

Advent Prayer

Father, in the wilderness of the Jordan,
you sent a messenger to prepare people's hearts
for the coming of your Son.
Help me to hear his words and repent of my sins,
so that I may clearly see the way to walk,
the truth to speak,
and the life to live for him,
Our Lord Jesus Christ.
Amen.

Jesse Tree

Heavenly Father, bless this tree, a reminder to us of your covenanted love, shown to your people, our ancestors, through the events of history in ancient times. May your son Christ, the shoot of Jesse, the true vine, invigorate us with his life and love, so that we may become his living branches in our world today. Amen.

The Veritas Book of Blessing Prayers

Christmas Crib Prayers

Heavenly Father,
As we wonder and hesitate to believe, like the
shepherds of Bethlehem, fill our hearts with joy,
as we recognise in this helpless babe the revelation
of your love, a new radiant vision of your glory.

Filled with wonder at the nearness of our God in
Mary's newborn child, may we now offer him our
praise, worship and thanksgiving and give him
the love and loyalty of our hearts. Amen.

The Veritas Book of Blessing Prayers

Father, you are Lord of heaven and earth.
You guide the stars; you have the whole world in
your hands;
you take care of all your people.
We thank you for all your gifts of love;
here today we thank you in a special way for this
crib.
We thank you for those who made it and for
those who erected it.
We thank you for leading us to praise you with
the help of this crib. We thank you most of all for
the birth of your Son.

We pray, Father, that you bless this crib. ✠
May it inspire all who pass by with the memory
of your love.
May it brighten the hearts of our people
and lighten their burden.
You have already done so much for us;
may the memory of this open our hearts to all the
great things you still want to do for us.
May there always be room in our hearts for your
Son, and for all your children in need.
Bless us with the peace the angels announced.
Teach us to recognise your Son as the shepherds
did.

May the light of your word guide us to him
as the star guided the wise men;
make us generous with the gifts you have given
us,
just as the wise men were generous.
Teach us to ponder all these things in our hearts,
as Mary did.

May we look forward with even greater joy to the
day when Jesus will come again, so that the whole
world may see the glory you have given him. He
now lives and reigns with you and the Holy
Spirit, one God, for ever and ever. Amen.

The Veritas Book of Blessing Prayers

Christmas

O God, who gladden us year by year
as we wait in hope for our redemption,
grant that, just as we joyfully welcome
your Only Begotten Son as our Redeemer,
we may also merit to face him confidently
when he comes again as our Judge.
Who lives and reigns with you in the unity of the
Holy Spirit,
one God, for ever and ever.

Collect, *Roman Missal,* 3rd edition

Blessing of the New Year; Be With Us, Lord

In *January*, the month of darkness and frost – Be with us, Lord

In *February*, the month of rain, wind and snow – Be with us, Lord

In *March*, the month of farmers, lambs and new life – Be with us, Lord

In *April*, the month of swallows, growth and green grass – Be with us, Lord

In *May*, the month of the cuckoo, the flowers and summer – Be with us, Lord

In *June*, the month of examinations, the midsummer and sun – Be with us, Lord

In *July*, the month of holidays, the dry grass and summer's end – Be with us, Lord

In *August*, the month of harvest, wheat and corn – Be with us, Lord

In *September*, the month of fruits, schools and St Michael – Be with us, Lord

In *October*, the month of falling leaves, nuts and Halloween – Be with us, Lord

In *November*, the month of the dead, the souls and the saints – Be with us, Lord

In *December*, the month of the gift, the light and Our Saviour – Be with us, Lord

Jubilee Resources, Archdiocese of Dublin

New Year Prayer

>God our Father,
>On this Feast of Mary, the Mother of God
>Give us an appreciation of the many gifts
>You have given us during the past year.
>Help us bless you in return during the coming
>year
>By sharing some of our gifts with others who have
>far, far less than we do.
>Amen.

Daily Lenten Prayer

Today Lord, I choose life,
I choose your love and the challenge to live it and
share it,
I choose hope, even in moments of darkness,
I choose faith, accepting you as Lord and God,
I choose to let go of some part of my burdens,
day by day handing them over to you,
I choose to take hold of your strength and power
ever more deeply in my life.
May this truly be for me a time of new life, of
change, challenge and growth.
May I come to Easter with a heart open to dying
with you
and rising to your new life, day by day.
Amen.

Lent

O God, author of every mercy and of all
goodness,
who in fasting, prayer and almsgiving
have shown us a remedy for sin,
look graciously on this confession of our
lowliness,
that we, who are bowed down by our conscience,
may always be lifted up by your mercy.
Through our Lord Jesus Christ, your Son,
who lives and reigns with you in the unity of the
Holy Spirit,
one God, for ever and ever.

Collect, *Roman Missal,* 3rd edition

Easter Prayer

Heavenly Father and God of mercy,
We no longer look for Jesus among the dead,
For he is alive and has become the Lord of life.
From the waters of death
You raise us with him
And renew your gift of life within us.
Increase in our minds and hearts
The risen life we share with Christ,
And help us to grow as your people
Toward the fullness of eternal life with you.
We ask this through Christ our Lord.
Amen.

Easter

> O God, who on this day,
> through your Only Begotten Son,
> have conquered death
> and unlocked for us the path to eternity,
> grant, we pray, that we who keep
> the solemnity of the Lord's Resurrection
> may, through the renewal brought by your Spirit,
> rise up in the light of life.
> Through our Lord Jesus Christ, your Son,
> who lives and reigns with you in the unity of the
> Holy Spirit,
> one God, for ever and ever.
>
> Collect, Roman Missal, 3rd edition

Autumn

Blessed are you, Lord
God of all creation,
You give us the
Goodness of autumn.

Gabhaim buíochas leat a Dhia,
As gach rud atá beo,
Plandaí agus bláthanna,
Agus torthaí go leor,
Gabhaim buíochas leat a Dhia
Anois i lár an Fhómhair.

Alive-O/Beo Go Deo

Winter
    Trees are bare,
    Frost's in the air.
    Nothing seems to grow.
    God's love is there,
    God still takes care
    of the winter world I know

    A Dhia an Gheimhridh
    A Dhia an Gheimhridh
    Tá do dhomhan faoi shuan.
    Slán faoi do ghrá
    Chomh daingean is chomh buan.

Alive-O 2/Beo go Deo 2

Spring

Blessed are you, Lord,
God of all creation,
Blessed are you Lord,
God of the spring.
Blessed are you, Lord,
God of everything.

Is beannaithe thú, a Thiarna,
A Rí na cruinne.
Is beannaithe thú, a Thiarna,
A Rí an Earraigh.
Is beannaithe thú, a Thiarna.

Alive-O 2/Beo go Deo 2

Summer

> For the light of the sun in the sky.
> For the light which shines through the window.
> For the light that shines early in the morning.
> For the light that shines late in the evening.
> We give God thanks and praise.
>
> Solas na gréine sa spéir.
> An solas a scalann tríd an fhuinneog.
> An solas a scalann ar maidin.
> An solas a scalann tráthnona.
> Molaimid thú aus gabhaimid buíochas leat, a
> Dhia.

Alive-O 2/Beo go Deo 2

The Seasons of Our Love

In the springtime of our marriage grant us growth
and hope.
In our summertime grant us warmth and
celebration.
In our autumn grant us harvest and affirmation.
And in our winter grant us closeness and support.
In all the seasons of our marriage be our constant
companion,
the guest invited to our wedding who has
remained faithful and ever present.

We ask this through Christ, our Lord. Amen.

Stephen Cummins

The Church is a Home for Everyone

Loving God,
may the Church be always
a home and family for everyone,
especially those who labour
and are heavy laden.

Rev Peter Murphy,
inspired by John Paul II, *Familiaris Consortio*, n.85

Living Our Values

O God,
let me always live
the values of kindness,
constancy, goodness,
service, disinterestedness
and self-sacrifice
that are the most precious fruit
of love.

Rev Peter Murphy,
inspired by John Paul II, *Familiaris Consortio*, n.36

The Difference Between 'Having' and 'Being'

We are more precious
for who we are than
for what we have materially.

Help me, Lord, to be
enriched not only with
a sense of true justice,
which alone leads to a respect
for the personal dignity of each
individual but also and more powerfully
by a sense of true love,
understood as sincere concern
and unselfish service of others,
especially the poorest
and those in most need.

Rev Peter Murphy,
inspired by John Paul II, *Familiaris Consortio*, n.37

The Gift of Every Life from God
      Knowing that each human life,
      even if weak and suffering,
      is always a splendid gift
      of God's goodness.
      As members of Christ's body,
      the family of the Church in the world,
      in each human life
      we see the splendour
      of that 'yes', that 'amen'
      who is Christ himself.

Rev Peter Murphy,
inspired by John Paul II, *Familiaris Consortio*, n.36

Praise for the Gift of Life
    God of Love, we praise and thank you
    for the wonderful gift of life.
    Help us to cherish that gift in ourselves and in all
    whom we meet.
    Bless all children that they may know
    the joy of being alive and that we may
    help them towards a great future.
    Bless all young men and women,
    be with them through these years
    of change in their bodies, their priorities,
    their relationships so that nothing may damage
    their joy and their hope.
    Bless all couples preparing for marriage.
    Help them to cherish each other more every day.
    And give them the courage to put their love for
    each other first so that their lives may
    be full and their marriages happy.
    We ask this through Christ our Lord.
    Amen.
                                    Johnny Doherty CSsR

Be a Sign and Presence of the Love of Jesus

O God our Father, who with your Son and the
Holy Spirit,
live forever in the unity and the beauty of love, in
the Holy Family of Nazareth
you have made visible the most perfect image of
the Trinity on earth.

Renew with your grace Christian families and
communities,
help them to be united and open by living in
mutual love and love towards all people.
By this action they will be a sign and a presence
in the world of Jesus who is our Saviour.

We ask you this through the intercession of Mary,
mother of Jesus and of the Church and Saint
Joseph her spouse,
in the name of Jesus, your Son and our Lord.
Amen.

Rev Peter Murphy

Prayer for Marriage and the Family
    Loving God,
    The well-being of each person
    and of the human and Christian society
    is closely bound up with the healthy
    state of the community of marriage and family.

    As we cherish the witness of the partnership
    of marriage and family life, we pray for all who
    answer this special calling to love and to life in
    their joys, sacrifices and sorrows.

    We pray for the fostering of this vocation of
    married love united with the Lord in faith, hope,
    and charity.
    And for the encouragement always of a reverence
    for human life in its eternal destiny.

Rev Peter Murphy,
inspired by Second Vatican Council, Gaudium et spes, n.47ff

With a Love of Preference for the Most Disadvantaged

May I follow you Lord
in your special love for all,
the most vulnerable
and disadvantaged,
with special concern for
the hungry,
the poor,
the old,
the sick,
drug victims
and those who have no family.

Rev Peter Murphy,
inspired by John Paul II, *Familiaris Consortio*, n.47

For World Peace
    Eternal God,
    creator of the world,
    you establish the order which governs all the ages.
    Hear our prayer and give us peace in our time
    that we may rejoice in your mercy
    and praise you without end.
    We ask this through Christ our Lord. Amen.

    May the peace of God which passes all
    understanding keep your hearts and your minds
    in Christ Jesus. Amen.

The Veritas Book of Blessing Prayers

For Peace

> Lord God, our Father,
> you seek the welfare of your children
> and not their destruction:
> direct our wills towards the peace for which we
> yearn;
> and let there be peace among the nations,
> peace in our land,
> peace in our homes,
> and peace in our hearts;
> that we may know that peace
> which passes all understanding
> in Jesus Christ our Lord. Amen.
>
> God grant to the living, grace;
> to the departed, rest;
> to the Church, our country and all humanity,
> peace and concord;
> and to us and all his servants, life everlasting;
> and may almighty God bless us,
> the Father, the Son, ✠ and the Holy Spirit. Amen.

The Veritas Book of Blessing Prayers

❖ ❖ ❖

Prayers for Those Caring for the Aged

Pour out your blessings, Lord,
upon your faithful servant.
Grant her patience and courage in her daily task.
Fill her with the gift of love
to strengthen her in the work to which you have
called her.
Give her an understanding of your caring
presence,
so that at all times she may confidently
place her trust in you.
Forgive her failures and weaknesses
so that she may experience your gift of peace in
her life.
We ask this through Christ our Lord.

May almighty God bless you, the Father, and the
Son, ✠ and the Holy Spirit. Amen.

The Veritas Book of Blessing Prayers

God of all love and strength,
support your servants who care for the aged.
May they give courage and self-respect
to those who feel weak and helpless,
and joy and hope to the sad and lonely.
When their task seems hard and demanding,
fill them with a sense of your strength and love,
through Jesus Christ our Lord.
Amen.

The Veritas Book of Blessing Prayers

Litany for a Growth in Love

In our respect for the equal dignity
of all human persons, created in your image.
May we dwell in your love, O God.

In our openness to others, relating to all
as neighbours in solidarity.
May we dwell in your love, O God.

In our welcome for the stranger with the joy
of recognising in them the face of Christ.
May we dwell in your love, O God.

In our respect for differences.
May we dwell in your love, O God.

In our understanding that every person
is my brother and sister.
May we dwell in your love, O God.

Rev Peter Murphy, *World Day of the Sick Prayerbook,* 2013

50th International Eucharistic Congress Prayer
>Lord Jesus,
>You were sent by the Father
>to gather together those who are scattered.
>You came among us, doing good and bringing
>healing,
>announcing the Word of salvation
>and giving the Bread which lasts forever.
>Be our companion on life's pilgrim way.
>
>May your Holy Spirit inflame our hearts,
>enliven our hope and open our minds,
>so that together with our sisters and brothers in
>faith we may recognise you in the scriptures
>and in the breaking of bread.
>May your Holy Spirit transform us into one body
>and lead us to walk humbly on the earth,
>in justice and love,
>as witnesses of your resurrection.
>
>In communion with Mary,
>whom you gave to us as our Mother
>at the foot of the cross,
>through you
>may all praise, honour and blessing be to the
>Father
>in the Holy Spirit and in the Church,
>now and forever.
>Amen.

❖ ❖ ❖

The Call of the Bell

Loving God,
from the very beginning of time
your voice has called to us,
inviting us to live
lives of faith, in prayer,
reconciliation and in mission.
As we reflect on the pilgrim bell of the 50th
International Eucharistic Congress
calling us to prayer,
we pray that in our experience of the Eucharist,
strengthened by the Word and the Bread of Life,
we will always deepen our communion
with Christ and with one another. Amen.

Rev Peter Murphy, *World Day of the Sick Prayerbook,* 2013

God's Love Has Been Given to Us

God,
your love
has been
poured into
our hearts
through
the Holy Spirit
who has
been given to us.

Rev Peter Murphy,
inspired by John Paul II, *Familiaris Consortio*, n.63

We are Prophets of a Future Not Our Own

It helps, now and then,
to step back and take the long view.
This is what we are about:
we plant seeds that one day will grow.
We water seeds already planted,
knowing that they hold future promise.
We lay foundations
that will need further development.
We provide yeast that produces
effects beyond our capabilities.
We cannot do everything
and there is a sense of liberation in
realising that.
This enables us to do something,
and to do it very well.
It may be incomplete, but it is a beginning,
a step along the way,
an opportunity for God's grace
to enter and do the rest.
We may never see the end results,
but that is the difference
between the master builder
and the workers.
We are workers, not master builders,
ministers, not messiahs.
We are prophets of a future not our own.

Bishop Ken Untener of Saginaw
from a reflection entitled 'The Mystery of the Romero Prayer'

❖ ❖ ❖

A Creed to Live By

Don't undermine your worth by comparing yourself with others.

It is because we are different that each of us is special.

Don't set your goals by what other people deem important.

Only you know what is best for you.

Don't take for granted the things closest to your heart.

Cling to them as you would your life, for without them life is meaningless.

Don't let life slip through your fingers by living in the past or in the future.

By living your life one day at a time, you live all the days of your life.

Don't give up when you still have something to give.

Nothing is really over until the moment you stop trying.

Don't be afraid to admit that you are less than perfect.

It is this fragile thread that binds us together.

Don't be afraid to encounter risks.

It is by taking chances that we learn how to be brave.

Don't shut love out of your life by saying it's impossible to find.

The quickest way to receive love is to give love;
The fastest way to lose love is to hold it too
tightly;
And the best way to keep love is to give it wings.
Don't dismiss your dreams.
To be without dreams is to be without hope;
To be without hope is to be without purpose.
Don't run through life so fast that you forget not
only where you've been,
But where you're going.
Life is not a race,
But a journey to be savoured every step of the
way.

Nancye Sims

God in an Apron
    Supper was special that night.
    There was both a heaviness and a holiness
    hanging in the air.
    We couldn't explain the mood.
    It was sacred, yet sorrowful.
    Gathered around that table
    eating that solemn, holy meal
    seemed to us the most important meal
    we had ever sat down to eat …

    And then suddenly
    the One we loved startled us all.
    He got up from the table
    And put on an apron.
    Can you imagine how we felt?

    GOD IN AN APRON!

    Tenderness encircled us
    as he bowed before us.
    He knelt and said,
    'I choose to wash your feet
    because I love you.'

    God in an apron, kneeling.
    I couldn't believe my eyes.
    I was embarrassed
    until his eyes met mine.
    I sensed my value then.

    He touched my feet,
    He held them in his strong brown hands.
    He washed them.

I can still feel the water.
I can still feel the touch of his hands.
I can still see the look in his eyes.

Then He handed me the towel and said
'As I have done, so you must do.'
Learn to bow. Learn to kneel.

Macrina Wiederkehr

Through the Year

Alone with none but thee, my God,
I journey on my way;
What need I fear, when thou art near,
O King of night and day?
More safe am I within thy hand,
Than if a host did round me stand.

My destined time is fixed by thee,
And Death doth know his hour.
Did warriors strong around me throng,
They could not stay his power;
No walls of stone can man defend
When thou thy messenger dost send.

My life I yield to thy decree,
And bow to thy control
In peaceful calm, for from thine arm
No power can wrest my soul.
Could earthly omens e'er appal
A man that heeds the heavenly call!

The child of God can fear no ill,
His chosen dread no foe;
We leave our fate with thee, and wait
Thy bidding when to go.
'Tis not from chance our comfort springs,
Thou art our trust, O King of kings.

Divine Office, Volume I, p. [242]

❖ ❖ ❖

APPENDIX ONE

GOD'S WORD AND MARRIAGE AND FAMILY

Marriage

Genesis 2:18, 24

The Lord God said, 'It is not right that the man should be alone. I shall make him a helper.' This is why a man leaves his father and mother and becomes attached to his wife, and they become one flesh.

Matthew 19:4-6

'Have you not read that the Creator from the beginning made them male and female and that he said: This is why a man leaves his father and mother and becomes attached to his wife, and the two become one flesh. They are no longer two, therefore, but one flesh. So then, what God has united, human beings must not divide.'

Proverbs 31:10-11

The truly capable woman – who can find her? She is far beyond the price of pearls. Her husband's heart has confidence in her; from her he will derive no little profit.

Ephesians 5:25

Husbands should love their wives, just as Christ loved the Church and sacrificed himself for her.

Ephesians 5:31-33

This is why a man leaves his father and mother and becomes attached to his wife, and the two become one flesh. This mystery has great significance, but I am applying it to Christ and the Church. To sum up: you also, each one of you, must love his wife as he loves himself; and let every wife respect her husband.

Genesis 2:23-24

And the man said, 'This one at last is bone of my bones and flesh of my flesh! She is to be called Woman, because she was taken from Man.' This is why a man leaves his father and mother and becomes attached to his wife, and they become one flesh.

Parenting

Ephesians 6:1-2

Children, be obedient to your parents in the Lord – that is what uprightness demands. The first commandment that has a promise attached to it is: Honour your father and your mother.

Colossians 3:21

Parents, do not irritate your children or they will lose heart.

Exodus 20:12

Honour your father and your mother so that you may live long in the land that the Lord your God is giving you.

Leviticus 19:32

You will stand up in the presence of grey hair; you will honour the person of the aged and fear your God. I am the Lord.

Matthew 19:13-15

The people brought little children to him, for him to lay his hands on them and pray. The disciples scolded them, but Jesus said, 'Let the little children alone, and do not stop them from coming to me; for it is to such as these that the kingdom of Heaven belongs.' Then he laid his hands on them and went on his way.

Psalm 103:13-14
As tenderly as a father treats his children, so the
Lord treats those who fear him; he knows what
we are made of, he remembers we are dust.

Family and Friends

Proverbs 27:9

Oil and perfume gladden the heart, and the sweetness of friendship rather than self-reliance.

1 Corinthians 15:34

So do not let anyone lead you astray, bad company corrupts good ways.

Proverbs 14:7

Keep well clear of the fool, you will not find wise lips there.

Proverbs 27:6

Trustworthy are blows from a friend, deceitful are kisses from a foe.

Proverbs 13:20

Whoever walks with the wise becomes wise, whoever mixes with fools will be ruined.

John 15:12-15

This is my commandment: love one another, as I have loved you. No one can have greater love than to lay down his life for his friends. You are my friends, if you do what I command you. I shall no longer call you servants, because a servant does not know the master's business; I call you friends, because I have made known to you everything I have learnt from my Father.

Psalm 128:1-6
Happy, all those who fear Yahweh and follow in
his paths. You will eat what your hands have
worked for, happiness and prosperity will be
yours. Your wife: a fruitful vine on the inner walls
of your house. Your sons: round your table like
shoots round an olive tree. Such are the blessings
that fall on the man who fears the Lord. May the
Lord bless you from Zion all the days of your life!
May you see Jerusalem prosperous and live to see
your children's children! Peace to Israel!

Ephesians 1:3
Blessed be God the Father of our Lord Jesus
Christ, who has blessed us with all the spiritual
blessings of heaven in Christ.

APPENDIX TWO

PRAYERS FROM THE CELEBRATION OF MARRIAGE

Nuptial Blessing (1)

Dear brothers and sisters,
let us humbly pray to the Lord
that on these his servants, now married in Christ,
he may mercifully pour out
the blessing of his grace
and make of one heart in love
(by the Sacrament of Christ's Body and Blood)
those he has joined by a holy covenant.

O God, who by your mighty power
created all things out of nothing,
and, when you had set in place
the beginnings of the universe,
formed man and woman in your own image,
making the woman an inseparable helpmate to
the man,
that they might no longer be two, but one flesh,
and taught that what you were pleased to make
one
must never be divided;
O God, who consecrated the bond of Marriage
by so great a mystery
that in the wedding covenant you foreshadowed
the Sacrament of Christ and his Church;

O God, by whom woman is joined to man
and the companionship they had in the beginning
is endowed with the one blessing
not forfeited by original sin
nor washed away by the flood.

Look now with favour on these your servants,
joined together in Marriage,
who ask to be strengthened by your blessing.
Send down on them the grace of the Holy Spirit
and pour your love into their hearts,
that they may remain faithful in the Marriage
covenant.

May the grace of love and peace
abide in your daughter N.,
and let her always follow the example of those
holy women
whose praises are sung in the Scriptures.
May her husband entrust his heart to her,
so that, acknowledging her as his equal
and his joint heir to the life of grace,
he may show her due honour
and cherish her always
with the love that Christ has for his Church.

And now, Lord, we implore you:
may these your servants
hold fast to the faith and keep your
commandments;
made one in the flesh,
may they be blameless in all they do;
and with the strength that comes from the
Gospel,
may they bear true witness to Christ before all;
(may they be blessed with children,
and prove themselves virtuous parents,
who live to see their children's children).

And grant that,
reaching at last together the fullness of years
for which they hope,
they may come to the life of the blessed
in the Kingdom of Heaven.
Through Christ our Lord.
Amen.

Roman Missal, 3rd edition

Nuptial Blessing (2)

Let us pray to the Lord for this bride and groom,
who come to the altar as they begin their married
life,
that (partaking of the Body and Blood of Christ)
they may always be bound together by love for
one another.

Holy Father,
who formed man in your own image,
male and female you created them,
so that as husband and wife, united in body and
heart,
they might fulfil their calling in the world;

O God, who, to reveal the great design you
formed in your love,
willed that the love of spouses for each other
should foreshadow the covenant you graciously
made with your people,
so that, by fulfilment of the sacramental sign,
the mystical marriage of Christ with his Church
might become manifest
in the union of husband and wife among your
faithful;

Graciously stretch out your right hand
over these your servants (N. and N.), we pray,
and pour into their hearts the power of the Holy
Spirit.

Grant, O Lord,
that, as they enter upon this sacramental union,
they may share with one another the gifts of your
love
and, by being for each other a sign of your presence,
become one heart and one mind.

May they also sustain, O Lord, by their deeds
the home they are forming
(and prepare their children
to become members of your heavenly household
by raising them in the way of the Gospel).

Graciously crown with your blessings your
daughter N.,
so that, by being a good wife (and mother),
she may bring warmth to her home with a love
that is pure
and adorn it with welcoming graciousness.

Bestow a heavenly blessing also, O Lord,
on N., your servant,
that he may be a worthy, good and
faithful husband (and a provident father).

Grant, holy Father,
that, desiring to approach your table
as a couple joined in Marriage in your presence,
they may one day have the joy
of taking part in your great banquet in heaven.
Through Christ our Lord.
Amen.

Roman Missal, 3rd edition

❖ ❖ ❖

Nuptial Blessing (3)

Let us humbly invoke by our prayers, dear
brothers and sisters,
God's blessing upon this bride and groom,
that in his kindness he may favour with his help
those on whom he has bestowed the Sacrament of
Matrimony.

Holy Father, maker of the whole world,
who created man and woman in your own image
and willed that their union be crowned with your
blessing,
we humbly beseech you for these your servants,
who are joined today in the Sacrament of
Matrimony.

May your abundant blessing, Lord,
come down upon this bride, N.,
and upon N., her companion for life,
and may the power of your Holy Spirit
set their hearts aflame from on high,
so that, living out together the gift of Matrimony,
they may (adorn their family with children
and) enrich the Church.

In happiness may they praise you, O Lord,
in sorrow may they seek you out;
may they have the joy of your presence
to assist them in their toil,
and know that you are near
to comfort them in their need;
let them pray to you in the holy assembly
and bear witness to you in the world,
and after a happy old age,
together with the circle of friends that surrounds
them,
may they come to the Kingdom of Heaven.
Through Christ our Lord.
Amen.

Roman Missal, 3rd edition

Solemn Blessing from the Celebration of Marriage
    May God the eternal Father
    keep you of one heart in love for one another,
    that the peace of Christ may dwell in you
    and abide always in your home.
    R: Amen.

    May you be blessed in your children,
    have solace in your friends
    and enjoy true peace with everyone.
    R: Amen.

    May you be witnesses in the world to God's charity,
    so that the afflicted and needy who have known
    your kindness
    may one day receive you thankfully
    into the eternal dwelling of God.

Roman Missal, 3rd edition

Collects from the Celebration of Marriage

Be attentive to our prayers, O Lord,
and in your kindness uphold
what you have established for the increase of the
human race,
so that the union you have created
may be kept safe by your assistance.
Through our Lord Jesus Christ, your Son,
who lives and reigns with you in the unity of the
Holy Spirit,
one God, for ever and ever.

O God, who in creating the human race
willed that man and wife should be one,
join, we pray, in a bond of inseparable love
these your servants who are to be united in the
covenant of Marriage,
so that, as you make their love fruitful,
they may become, by your grace, witnesses to
charity itself.
Through our Lord Jesus Christ, your Son,
who lives and reigns with you in the unity of the
Holy Spirit,
one God, for ever and ever.

Roman Missal, 3rd edition

Cross of St Brigid Blessing

Priest: The peace of the Father be with you.
The peace of Christ be with you.
The peace of the Spirit be with you.
Every day and every night. Amen.

People: Every day and night. Amen.

Priest: May the Father protect you.
May Christ protect you.
May the Spirit protect you.
Every day and night of your life. Amen.

People: Every day and night of our life. Amen.

Priest: The blessing of the Father come upon you.
The blessing of Christ come upon you.
The blessing of the Spirit come upon you.
Until you are crowned with eternal life.
Amen.

People: Until we are crowned with eternal life.
Amen.

Priest: May God prosper you
from Samhain to St Brigid's Day to May
Day,
from May Day to Lúnasa,
and from Lúnasa to Samhain,
and may almighty God bless you:
Father, Son and Holy Spirit.

People: Amen.

Priest: Go now, safe in the peace of Christ.

People: Thanks be to God.

A Wedding of Your Own

❖ ❖ ❖

Beannacht ag Deireach an Aifrinn

Sagart: Síochain an Athar libh,
         Síochain Chríost libh,
         Síochain an Spioraid libh,
         Gach lá agus oíche. Amen.

Pobal: Gach lá agus oíche. Amen.

Sagart: Coimirce an Athar oraibh,
         Coimirce Chríost oraibh,
         Coimirce an Spioraid oraibh,
         Gach lá agus oíche de bhur saol. Amen.

Pobal: Gach lá agus oíche de bhur saol. Amen.

Sagart: Beannacht an Athar oraibh,
         Beannacht Chríost oraibh,
         Beannacht an Spioraid oraibh,
         Go coróin na beatha síoraí. Amen.

Pobal: Go coróin na beatha síoraí. Amen.

Sagart: Bail ó Dhia oraibh ó Shamhain go Lá 'le
         Bride,
         ó Lá 'le Bride go Bealtaine,
         ó Bhealtaine go Lúnasa,
         is ó Lúnasa go Samhain;
         is go mbeannaí Dia uilechumhachtach sibh,
         Athair, Mac ✠ agus Spiorad Naomh.

Pobal: Amen.

Sagart: Go dté sibh slán faoi shíocháin Chríost.

Pobal: Buíochas le Dia.

Gnás an Phósta

ACKNOWLEDGEMENTS

Excerpts from the English translation of *The Roman Missal* © 2010, ICEL. All rights reserved.

Alive-O/Beo-go-Deo, Dublin: Veritas, 1996–2005.

Catholic Household Blessings and Prayers, Washington, DC: United States Conference of Catholic Bishops, 2007.

Doherty, Johnny CSsR, *Ask, Search, Knock: A Movement of Continuous Prayer for Marriage and Family Life*, Southeastern PA: Pastoral and Matrimonial Renewal Center, 2000.

Fitzgerald, M., OFM, ed., *Catholic Book of Prayers*, Totowa, NJ: Catholic Book Publishing Corporation, 2011.

Gnás an Phósta, Dublin: Veritas, 1980.

McCarthy, Pádraig, *A Wedding of Your Own*, 4th edition Dublin: Veritas, 2003.

Prayerbook for Those Affected by Addiction, Dublin: Pastoral Response to Substance Misuse Initiative of the Irish Bishops' Conference, 2013.

Prayers inspired by John Paul II, *Familiaris Consortio*, The Christian Family in the Modern World, and by Vatican II, *Gaudium et spes*, © Rev Peter Murphy

The Celebration of Marriage Within Mass, Dublin: Veritas, 2011.

The Glenstal Book of Prayer, Dublin: Columba Press, 2001.

The Notre Dame Book of Prayer, Notre Dame, IN: Ave Maria Press, 2010. 'Prayer for an Engaged Couple' by Kathy and Kevin Misiewicz, copyright 2010 by the University of Notre Dame Office of Campus Ministry. Notre Dame, IN 46556. Used with permission of the publisher.

The Veritas Book of Blessing Prayers, Dublin: Veritas, 1989.

Wiederkehr, Macrina, *Seasons of Your Heart: Prayers and Reflections*, New York: HarperOne, 1991.

World Day of the Sick Prayerbook, Dublin: Archdiocese of Dublin, 2013.

YOUCAT: Youth Prayer Book, San Francisco: Ignatius Press, 2013.

Online Sources
Catholic Online, www.catholic.org

Prayerbook: A Catholic Religious Site,
    www.prayerbook.com, © Geo M. Haney Jr, The
    Prayer Book Ministry.